How to Advertise

How to Advertise

By
Kenneth Roman
and Jane Maas

St. Martin's Press

Library of Congress Catalogue #74-24835
ISBN 0-312-39550-7
ISBN: 0-312-39585-X
Manufactured in the United States of America
No part of this book may be reproduced without
permission in writing from the publisher.

St. Martin's Press, 175 Fifth Avenue, New York, N.Y. 10010

AFFILIATED PUBLISHER: Macmillan Limited, London
—also at Bombay, Calcutta, Madras and Melbourne

Designed by Tony Esposito

To our expert teachers

and our patient families

Contents

Foreword

If you aspire to become a good doctor or a good lawyer, you can learn a lot by reading textbooks.

But if you aspire to become a good advertising man (or woman), you cannot learn from textbooks because there aren't any good ones. So you have to learn everything on the job.

There are two things wrong with this. First, it takes half a lifetime (as in my own case). Second, you will be lucky if you can find a boss who knows enough to teach you anything.

Here, at last, is a book from which you can learn a lot about the practical business of advertising. When you have read it, you will know what it took me twenty-five years to learn on the job. Lucky you.

Everything in the book bears out what I have learned. It is all valid information, worth its weight in gold.

Ken Roman and Jane Maas, who wrote it, know what they are talking about. From experience.

Ken is in charge of a very big advertising account, with a team of 24 executives under his command. He also understands the problems which face clients; he was once a client himself.

Jane Maas is a copywriter—and an avid student of advertising. She has made it her business to study the factors which make some campaigns succeed, while others fail. And, like Ken, she is uncommonly sensitive to the role of the client-agency partnership, from which all good advertising is born.

ix

How to Get Great Advertising

"I HAPPENED TO HAVE some research which showed that a wonderful factor to have in the illustration of any advertisement was 'story appeal.' So I thought of 22 different story-appeal elements to put in the photograph of the Hathaway shirts. The twenty-second of them was the eyepatch. It turned out to be a good idea. *But I would not have gone looking for it if I didn't know the research.*"

David Ogilvy relates the birth of his campaign for Hathaway: the result of hard work, knowing the rules, and creative brilliance.

This book is a *professional* guide for the advertiser—the one person who must make the final decision . . . and spend the money.

It is a book, too, for students of advertising, who have much information about marketing, but little about the creative process.

Hard work. Knowing the rules. Creative brilliance. That's the advertising philosophy of this book.

Start with the rules: a knowledge of what usually works . . . and what doesn't. Follow them too slavishly, and you will end up with demoralized creative people and mediocre advertising. Treat each rule in this book as a guideline, a place to *begin*. Read every affirmation as a question.

Do rules inhibit creative people? Shakespeare was not inhibited by the sonnet form, nor Beethoven by the symphony. Robert Frost complained about the lack of discipline in writing free verse: "It's like playing tennis with the net down."

This book will tell you how to *look* at advertising, not how to write it. How to position your product—the first and most important decision. How to tell whether a storyboard will make a good commercial, and what dramatic techniques work best in television.

There are guidelines for print, radio, outdoor and direct mail advertising. How to get better media planning, better research, better production. There are suggestions on how to be a better client, and how to encourage truthful and responsible advertising.

This book is unique in two respects. It is the first book *for advertisers* (not advertising writers) *about copy* (not marketing). The *you* in the book refers to you, the advertiser. Some things are clearly your responsibility—setting a marketing goal, for instance. Others will be done by the copywriter or account executive or media planner. You won't do these yourself, but you should know if they have been done well.

The creation of advertising is a *joint* venture. The joint authorship of this book—an account man and a copywriter—is testimony to that attitude.

The partnership extends to the advertiser. You are an integral part of the creative process. You can help. Or you can hurt. The more you know about creativity, the more you will help and the greater the chance you will get great advertising.

David Ogilvy often counsels his agency colleagues: "Do not grudge your client the right to contribute ideas and criticism. It is his product, his money and his responsibility."

KENNETH ROMAN
JANE MAAS
New York, 1975

Chapter I

How to Position a Product or Service

ADVERTISING OFTEN BORROWS the language of war. We wage *campaigns*. We *aim* the advertising at a *target* audience. We *launch* products like missiles and force the competition to react with a *defense plan*.

Ulysses S. Grant, asked to define the art of war, said, "I do not believe in luck in war any more than luck in business." Successful advertising, like a military victory, is usually the result of careful *planning*.

In advertising, the first planning decision is also the most important: *How to position your product.* Positioning has recently become a fashionable word. Everyone agrees it's important, but there's a lot of argument about exactly what it *is*. Advertising theorists are behaving like the judge who said, "I can't define pornography. But I know it when I see it."

You know, when you see automobile advertising, that one car is clearly a luxury car—because of its styling. Another is a sensible family car. A third is a high-performance sports car. Distinctly different positions.

The dictionary says that position is "the place held by a person or thing." When you position your product, you *place it a certain way in the consumer's mind.*

1

Once you have made that all-important decision, you need a *strategy* (another military term!) to get you there.

The *marketing strategy* is the master plan. It spawns several substrategies (for packaging, pricing and media) that guide different aspects of your planning. The *creative strategy* (also known as the copy, or advertising, strategy) determines what you say in the advertising, and how you will say it.

Let's look at an example of positioning: Dove beauty bar.

In 1957, Lever Brothers decided to position a new product as a complexion bar for dry skin, not as a soap to get you clean. The Dove *marketing strategy* reflects that position.

> *The name "Dove" fits a beauty bar. The oval shape is more feminine than the traditional soap rectangle. Dove comes in a box, like a cosmetic, instead of a paper wrapper. It is clearly a product for women.*

From the marketing strategy grew the *creative strategy*—how the advertising would persuade women that Dove is better than soap.

Dove's print and television advertising contrasted the effects of Dove and soap by showing pretty women taking the "Dove Face Test." Advertising promised that Dove "creams your skin while you wash," and supported that promise with a demonstration of the cleansing cream pouring into the bar.

Dove has held its positioning for 18 years. The strategy has never changed. Every commercial still uses the cleansing cream demonstration.

2

Creative strategies differ in form and terminology, but a good one must cover five key points.

1. **Objective**—what the advertising should do.

2. **Target audience**—who is your consumer?

3. **Key consumer benefit**—why the consumer should buy your product.

4. **Support**—a reason to believe in that benefit.

5. **Tone and manner**—a statement of the product "personality."

How to Build a Creative Strategy

"Thinking is the hardest work many people ever have to do, and they don't like to do any more of it than they can help," wrote Robert R. Updegraff in his business classic, *Obvious Adams*. "They look for a royal road through some short cut in the form of a clever scheme or stunt, which they call the obvious thing to do; but calling it doesn't make it so. They don't gather all the facts and then analyze them before deciding what is really the obvious thing, and thereby they overlook the first and most obvious of all business principles."

Immerse yourself in facts. Study the market, the product, the competition, the consumer.

Understanding the market in depth is the first step in building a strategy.

At this stage, you're beginning to identify the best prospects for a product. The next step is to determine what consumer benefits are important or unique to this audience.

3

Organize facts into hypotheses. Generate new hypotheses with qualitative research—focused group sessions or depth interviews. Consider creative hunches along with logical deductions. *All ideas are good ones at this point.*

Test the most promising ideas. (More about strategy development research later.) Use testing to select a winner around which you can build a strategy.

Not a complicated process. But, as Obvious Adams puts it, "Advertising is not white magic, but, like everything else, just plain common sense."

17 Strategy Checkpoints

Here are some tips to keep in mind as you and your agency hammer out a creative strategy.

1. Make the creative strategy fit the marketing plan.

Don't let the product, price, and package go off in one direction, while the advertising goes off in another. The team must work in harness.

If you are selling an automobile that is superbly engineered, your creative strategy should demand advertising that shows how the car performs on the road, not how beautiful it looks in your driveway.

2. Keep your objectives reasonable.

Overambition is the pitfall of most strategies. Don't try to talk to everyone (instead of likely users), don't sell a product for all occasions, don't ask people to change their habits (instead of just their brand). Changing deeply ingrained habits may be the hardest job for advertising.

4

*Women have come to use hair-coloring openly, as
a cosmetic. Those few men who touch up gray
hair are reluctant to admit it. Despite heavy
advertising, men's attitudes—and habit
patterns—have changed little.*

3. Make your strategy easy to use.

It should be very short, very sharp, and leave no
room for misunderstanding. *One page*—with as much
backup rationale as you need.

*Winston Churchill sent this directive to the First
Lord of the Admiralty: "Pray state this day, on
one side of a sheet of paper, how the Royal Navy
is being adapted to meet the conditions of modern
warfare."*

4. Be single-minded.

Great ideas are simple. Give the copywriter clear,
single-minded direction if you expect a big idea to reach
the consumer.

Agree on what is most important. Everything
about your product is important—to you. To consumers, some product characteristics are more important
than others. Time spent talking about minor copy
points will blur communication of your main consumer
benefit.

5. State a business objective.

What do you want the consumer to *do* after hearing your message? Are you looking for new people to
try your product, or for regular purchasers to use it
more often?

*Recipe advertising usually means the strategy
aims to build usage of a product already in the*

> *home. Hershey offers special recipes like
> "Hand-Me-Down" cake to encourage women to
> use more Hershey's Cocoa in cooking.*

The strategy has at its heart a clear statement of the problem to be solved.

6. Decide where your business is going to come from.

Unless you have a unique new product that brings new consumers into the market, your business generally comes out of someone else's business. Strategies should recognize the source.

> *Lean Strips, a meatless bacon, is positioned as a
> less-expensive bacon replacement. This product,
> which looks and tastes like bacon, will get its
> business from people who like bacon, not from
> people looking for a new kind of taste.*

7. Understand your target audience.

Most strategies spend too much time on product attributes, too little on the consumer. Go beyond age and income. Define attitudes and usage patterns that will help the copywriter talk to the most likely buyer.

Write a one-page profile of your consumer. Is she a young airline hostess who lives in an urban apartment, or a suburban mother of three? This exercise helps you see your buyer as an individual—not a mass.

8. Make a meaningful promise to the consumer.

"Promise, large promise, is the soul of an advertisement," said Dr. Samuel Johnson. Your product's benefit to the consumer must be meaningful and strong if the advertising is to do its job.

*Aim toothpaste has several consumer benefits: a
taste children like, as well as stannous fluoride
and a gel formula that spreads fast. These benefits
are summarized in the promise: "Take Aim
against cavities."*

9. Support your promise.

Do something to make your promise convincing.
Former agency head Jack Tinker once estimated that
over a billion dollars had been spent advertising each of
these six adjectives: new, white, cool, power, refreshing,
relief. Why should the housewife believe *you?*

*"Burpee seeds grow"—a classically simple
promise—is backed by a standing offer:
"Satisfaction guaranteed or your money back."*

10. Set yourself apart.

Look for an empty niche in the market. Avoid positioning that is *exactly* the same as your competitor's. If
you want to be in the same general area as your competition, build in some element that will set your brand
apart.

*Spray 'n Vac entered the rug shampoo market
with a product that cleaned rugs without
scrubbing. Commercials that demonstrated this
unique advantage helped Spray 'n Vac lead the
category within six months after introduction.*

The A. C. Nielsen Company has studied the introduc-
tions of hundreds of new products. They conclude that
the *second* product introduced in a market typically will
get only *half* the share of the pioneer brand. To over-
come this pattern, the second advertiser must either
spend significantly more—or have a significantly better
product.

11. Give your product a distinctive personality.

It is very hard to do. Many products never achieve a "brand image" of their own. This personality goes beyond the product itself; it is an aura that helps set your brand apart from all others.

> *The brand image of Schweppes Tonic Water goes beyond the adult taste of the product or its English origin. It is an elitist image that verges on snobbery.*

Every advertisement you run should contribute to the long-term image of your brand.

12. Advertise what is important, not what is obvious.

Gallup & Robinson research shows that many advertisements waste their breath talking about product benefits that are quickly apparent. The right strategy is to talk about important benefits not so apparent.

> *Moist dog foods are more convenient than canned. That's obvious. What's important is whether the dog will eat them.*

13. Think ahead.

Being first is best. Being first with something your competitors will take a long time to imitate—a preemptive element—is best of all. Don't underestimate your competition.

> *Shell No-Pest Strip became a market leader with an effective and unique insecticide, packaged in a decorator dispenser.*

14. Keep your strategy up to date.

The world changes. So does your market and your

consumer. Parts of your strategy—the key benefit and the personality—should almost never change, and then only with a real understanding of the implications of a new positioning. But as you get new information, polish the strategy and keep it up to date.

> *People who try new products are younger, better educated, richer, and more venturesome than the average. They tend to try your new product, and then go on and try someone else's—often leaving you with a different group of customers than you started with.*

15. Don't change your strategy without good reason.

Falling sales could result from poor executions of a good strategy. Or new competition in the market. Take a hard look at *all* aspects of your business before you think about changing your strategy. Then, test.

> *Crystal Drāno, on a strategy of germ-free drains, was losing share to the newer, liquid drain cleaners. Women were more concerned about clogs than germs. Drāno successfully turned to a competitive strategy that promised faster unclogging.*

16. Put the strategy in writing.

It's easy to fall in love with a new campaign, and forget the discipline of positioning. Get your strategy statement in writing, and refer to it. The first question to be asked of any advertisement is: "Is it on strategy?"

17. Have a better product.

Too many business and advertising people are so convinced of the power of advertising that they believe it can sell anything. While great advertising can give products a place in the market, usually there is a real product advantage behind marketing successes. Better advertising starts with a better product.

Before You Look at Advertising, Review the Strategy

Remind yourself of the strategy you and the agency have agreed upon. Remember that you have already identified your target audience, your consumer benefit, or promise, and the support for that promise.

Now look at the advertising. If it does not conform to the strategy, reject it. You will never have an easier or better reason to turn down creative work. It may be brilliant, compelling advertising, but if it is off strategy, you must be ruthless. *Turn it down.*

There are no exceptions to this rule.

You must also reject advertising that conflicts with your brand's personality, the image you have decided to create.

If your food product has established an image of old-fashioned goodness, you should not accept a commercial with a rock music track, no matter what the words say.

There are no exceptions to this rule either. Brand personalities are too hard-won to be sacrificed to the whim of one advertisement.

The results of your advertising depend less on how your advertising is written than on how your product or service is positioned—how you want the consumer to think about it. The strategy is the instrument to get you there.

At best, the discipline of a strategy makes good creative work better. At the very least, it can transform even mediocre executions into selling tools.

Just as in war, the strategy is half the battle. The other half is the advertising itself. That's the subject from here on.

¼ cleansing cream

A demonstration helps position Dove beauty bar.

A white rum martini?

New drinks build usage for Puerto Rican rum.

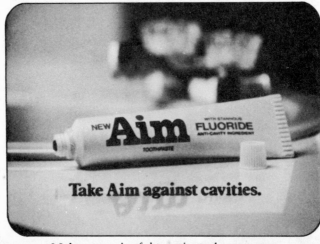

Take Aim against cavities.

Make a meaningful promise to the consumer.

Chapter II

What Works Best in Television

W HAT DO YOU DO if your agency shows you a commercial that is on strategy—*and you don't like it* (but you don't know why)? Where do you turn for guidance in this very subjective area?

This chapter will deal with the two basic questions you should ask:

1. Is the commercial *effective?*

2. What is the best *dramatic technique* for the product and the strategy?

How can you look at a storyboard and know whether the commercial is good?

Not pretty. Not entertaining. Not award winning.

Good means *effective.* It is nice to have advertising that charms the consumer, as long as it persuades her to buy.

How do you know a commercial is going to sell? Here is a checklist to help you judge a storyboard.

But first, what *is* a storyboard?

How to Look at a Storyboard

It can come in many forms and sizes—horizontal, vertical, single pictures in a "flip chart" style. Most storyboards have three important elements: *pictures* that indicate the main action of the commercial, and a written description of what the viewer will see *(the video)* and hear *(the audio)*.

Technical terms in storyboards

There are few you really need to know. A *dissolve* is a leisurely change of pace that indicates passage of time. A *cut* is a fast change of action: film can cut from a man's hand to his face. A *long shot* would show all of a spokesman; a *medium shot* just his head and shoulders; a *close-up* (or *CU*) his head alone; and an *extreme close-up* (or *ECU*) just his eyes. *V.O.* means *voice over*, as opposed to *D.V.*, a *direct voice* on camera. *SFX* are sound effects or music.

There is one simple rule for looking at a storyboard. *Always look at the pictures first.* Are they telling the story? *Then,* look at the words.

Now you're ready to decide if the storyboard will make an effective commercial.

10 Ways to Get a More Effective Commercial

1. The picture must tell the story.

Forget every other rule in this chapter, and you will still be ahead of the game. It's the most important rule of all! Yet time after time, in presenting storyboards to advertising professionals, we see their eyes shift to the column where the *words* are.

Television is a *visual* medium. That's why the people in front of a set are called *viewers*. They remember what they *see,* not what they hear.

Try this trick for looking at a storyboard. *Cover the words.* What is the message of the commercial with the sound turned off? Is there a message at all?

When you look at a storyboard, look at the pictures *first.* Ask yourself if they are telling the story.

2. Look for a "key visual."

Here's another test to apply to the storyboard. Can you pick out *one* frame that visually sums up the whole message? Most good commercials can be reduced to this single "key visual."

> *One key visual easily expresses the Merrill Lynch campaign. It is a herd of bulls thundering toward camera, with the title: "Merrill Lynch is bullish on America."*

A commercial with many different scenes may look interesting in storyboard form, but can turn out to be an overcomplicated piece of film. Busy, crowded, fast-moving commercials are hard to understand. The small television screen is not a movie theatre.

A *simple* storyboard can fool you. It may look hopelessly dull on paper. But film thrives on simplicity.

3. Grab the viewer's attention.

The *first five seconds* of a commercial are crucial. Analysis of audience reaction shows either a sharp drop or a sharp rise in interest during the first five seconds. *Commercial attention does not build.* Your audience can only become less interested, never more. The level you reach in the first five seconds is the highest you will get, so don't save your punches.

> *"You are about to witness a crime!" That's the attention-grabbing opening of commercials for American Express Travelers Cheques. The viewer sees a pocket picked before his eyes. This campaign about the dangers of carrying cash helped American Express increase sales 28 percent.*

Offer the viewer something right off the bat. *News*. A *problem* to which you have the solution. A *conflict* that is involving.

4. Be single-minded.

A good commercial is uncomplicated. Direct. It never makes the viewer do a lot of mental work.

The basic commercial length in U.S. television is 30 seconds. The content possible in that time is outlined in the phrase: "name-claim-demonstration." The name of your product, your consumer benefit, and the reason the consumer should believe it.

> *Premium Saltine crackers introduced their new moisture-proof Polybag wrapper with a single-minded commercial. A little boy accidentally drops a packet in the ocean and returns to pick it up. His satisfied crunch demonstrates that the crackers are still crisp.*

Longer commercials *should not add copy points.* A 60-second commercial tells the same story as the 30-second one, with more leisure and detail. Or—best of all—*repetition*. The 60-second allows time for a mood to be created; the 30-second generally does not.

16

The 20-second and 10-second commercials are one-point messages. The 10-second registers the brand name and promise. The 20-second makes the promise more explicit. Both these lengths are usually *reminder* messages, run in a media schedule with longer commercial lengths.

If your campaign plans include both :60s and :30s, ask the agency to show you the :30s *first*. If the message cannot be delivered in 30 seconds, you are not being single-minded.

5. Register the name of your product.

Too often, a viewer will remember the commercial but not the name of your brand. This is a problem particularly troublesome with new products. Showing the package on screen and mouthing the name is not enough. Take extra pains to implant your product name in the viewer's mind.

> *Glade air freshener drove home the name of its new scent, Fresh Herbal, by making the name a game. A man named Herb and his wife argue about the pronunciation—Herbal versus Erbal. Finally, the frustrated wife cries: "It's Erbal, Erb!" Viewers remembered the name.*

6. Show people, not objects.

People are interested in people. You will have a more memorable commercial—and register more key copy points—if you show a person *on camera* with your product instead of the product in limbo with a disembodied voice-over.

7. Have a payoff.

Show that your product does what you said it will—a "moment of affirmation." At some point, the housewife should admire the whiter wash, the shaver should stroke his smooth cheek, the dog should eat the dog food.

8. The tone of your advertising must reflect your product personality.

If you are fortunate enough to have a product with an established brand image, your advertising *must* reflect that image.

It takes dedication on the part of advertiser and agency to build a brand personality. Discipline yourself to reject advertising that conflicts with it. (It helps to have a written "personality statement" of your product; if it were a person, what sort of person would it be?)

When you launch a new product, the very *tone* of your announcement commercial tells viewers what to expect. From that moment on, it is hard to change their minds.

Once you have decided on a personality for your product, sustain it in every commercial. Change campaigns when you must, but retain the same tone of voice.

9. Avoid "talky" commercials.

Look for the simplest, and most memorable, set of words to get across your consumer benefit. Every word must work hard.

A 30-second commercial usually allows you *no more* than 65 words, a 60-second commercial twice that amount. Be specific. Pounce upon clichés, flabbiness, and superlatives.

Try this discipline. When you ask for ten words to be added to a commercial, decide which ten you would *delete* to make room for them.

18

10. Build campaigns, not individual commercials.

When you look at new advertising for your brand, be sure the storyboard is based on a *big idea.* You will want to film many commercials on the same theme to build a campaign. Successful advertising says the same thing over and over, with slight variations.

There's one fast way to tell if a commercial will extend into a campaign. Look at the storyboard, and pretend *you* are going to have to write the next advertisement in the "pool."

What's the Best Dramatic Technique for Your Product and Your Story?

Your agency has just recommended a testimonial commercial. You think a stand-up presenter is a better idea. Who is right? The decision is *not* totally subjective.

Television commercials can come in many dramatic forms. Strict definitions are arbitrary, but there are six *basic* techniques. Each one has a unique strength. One may be more appropriate than another for your product.

Technique #1: Demonstrations—when you can show a product advantage.

Television must have been invented with the demonstration in mind. If you can show that your product does something well, or better than competition, *show it.* And show it in every commercial you run.

There are all kinds of demonstrations. A car driving over a bed of nails with its tires intact. A housewife showing her friend how fast a paper towel soaks up spills. You can devote all of your commercial to a demonstration, or just part of it.

> *Demonstrations don't have to be dull.*
> *International Paper demonstrated the strength of paper with an imaginative torture test: they spanned a canyon with a bridge made of paperboard and drove a truck over it.*

The demonstration will be the most memorable part of your commercial. Make sure you are proving a point that is *important* to the consumer.

When you can't film the real thing (stomach acid) or want to simplify a complex story (atomic energy) you can use a *symbolic demonstration*.

> *The first commercial for Maxim coffee used symbols to introduce freeze-drying. It showed coffee brewed in a percolator, frozen into a block, reduced to crystals in a bell jar. Simple symbols of the complex equipment that makes freeze-dried coffee.*

If you can, always *show* the viewer what your product does.

Technique #2: Testimonials—when you want to make a claim believable.

There is an authenticity about testimonials that actors cannot duplicate. An awkward pause, tangled syntax, a clearing of the throat. Testimonials say to the viewer: "This is the truth." They are particularly appropriate when you cannot visualize a product advantage. The consumer *might* take the advertiser's word that the product smells or tastes better. She is more likely to believe the word of a fellow consumer.

Like demonstrations, testimonials have great variety.

• *Celebrity endorsements.* Very effective when the celebrity has relevance to the product.

> *Sears, Roebuck used fashion designer Bonnie Cashin to endorse the features of its sewing machine.*

• *Endorsements by experts.* The expert may be a well-known person, like a racing car driver for Shell Oil, or just an average consumer with a particular knowledge of the product.

• *Testimonials by ordinary people.* People who are clearly not actors say good things about your product in their own words. Enormous believability!

> *Shell gave its testimonials a reverse twist by disguising an interviewer as a gas station attendant. He tried to talk drivers out of buying Super Shell. The users' passionate defense was convincing testimony.*

(New film techniques can help give the testimonial a fresh look. *Cinéma vérité* uses hand-held cameras and available light. The people know they are being filmed, but tend to ignore the camera.)

When you look at a storyboard for a testimonial, remember that the finished commercial will probably be quite different. The best testimonials happen when real people say unexpected things that a writer would never dream of. Storyboards of testimonials often look dull. It is the aura of reality that gives life to the film.

> *A legal note: You must be able to document that a consumer actually uses and likes your product*

before you ask him to appear in a commercial. The most common method is using an independent research organization to find enthusiastic product users.

Technique #3: Presenters—when you have product news.

The stand-up salesman was the original television commercial. It is still the standby for small, local television advertisers because this kind of commercial is simple. And cheap. The strength of the stand-up presenter format is that it says *news*—even if there is no news.

This technique depends largely on the effectiveness of the presenter. There are celebrity presenters, created personalities, heads of companies, and actors in business suits.

The best presenter is one who goes beyond the product message—and helps build an image for the brand.

Pete the butcher has become a memorable, authoritative spokesman for Shake 'n Bake coating mix. This campaign helped create a new business that has grown consistently and dramatically.

You can use established celebrities, from entertainment or sports. Sheer fame or memorability is not enough. Choose a presenter who is *relevant* to your product.

One "personality screening" test showed that a world-famous actress was memorable, but would not have persuaded women to buy the product.

Do people remember the celebrity or the product? Research shows that the celebrity is usually *more effective in registering copy points*. The viewer is paying attention.

22

(Remember, the celebrity is mortal. He or she can get sick, fall from public favor, or make a pornographic movie. Have a backup campaign ready.)

Sometimes, a celebrity can be *created* by putting the head of a company in front of a television camera. (Few people have the presence that the spokesman role demands. Never volunteer yourself. *Think twice if your agency asks you to do it.*)

Technique #4: The slice-of-life—when you want to involve people with your product.

It's based on the oldest dramatic technique there is— actors telling a story. No wonder the slice works so well! A little play unfolds, involving the people with the product. And the product usually holds center stage.

Some creative people don't much like the slice-of-life. They consider it corny. Yet it can be highly memorable and persuasive.

There are a number of elements that make one slice better than another.

• *Simplicity:* Concentrate on a single product benefit. The slice-of-life is like a biblical parable, very simple and easily remembered.

• *Problem/Solution:* Set up a human problem that your product solves. Conflict often increases viewer involvement. The classic slice always shows conversion, the "doubter" convinced.

• *"Authority figure":* The character who delivers your message must be relevant to your product. Many successful campaigns have been built on the authority figure as a *continuing* character.

Maxwell House is the only coffee sold in Cora's

*country store. When customers complain about
their coffee problems, Cora has the answer on her
shelf. This advertising helped Maxwell House
hold its national leadership in the coffee market.*

• *Demonstration:* Done within the context of the slice-of-life, it can make the claims more believable.

• *Serious tone of voice:* The slice-of-life works best when it is serious, not whimsical or funny. Humor tends to lower its effectiveness.

• *A mnemonic device:* Sometimes called a *relevant symbol,* it's a way to dramatize your product benefit within a slice. For years, doves flew into kitchens to symbolize the gentleness of Dove for Dishes.

Technique #5: Life-style advertising—to focus attention on the user, rather than on the product.

This kind of advertising works best when product differences are small and when the product's use tends to be social (not just functional).

*Tijuana Smalls, a little cigar, was aimed at
younger men who smoked cigarettes. The
advertising focused on the contemporary man
smoking it. Each commercial asked the viewer:
"For you? Maybe. You know who you are." It was
the most successful new product introduction in
the cigar business.*

Technique #6: Animation—for special communication purposes.

Animation is especially effective—and widely used—to talk to children. They enjoy and remember cartoon characters.

An animated campaign for Burger Chef
restaurants features two characters, "Burger Chef
and Jeff," who have visitors like Count
Fangburger, Burgerilla the ape and Burgerini
the magician. Awareness and attitudes among
children rose sharply with this advertising.

Animation is an effective solution for other problems—simplifying complex ideas (often in demonstrations), or treating abstract or even distasteful subjects.

Some Notes on Entertainment

Many of the most popular and best-liked commercials have gone off the air because they failed to sell the product. Some of the longest-running campaigns regularly make the "ten most hated" list, and represent the top selling brands. *There is no correlation between entertainment value and sales results.*

Humor, music, and sex are additional fillips that can be added to just about any commercial, no matter what the technique. *Beware. They may blur your sales message.*

Use this test. Can you remove the sales message from a commercial, and still have a commercial? If you *can*, entertainment is getting in the way.

Humor: when it contributes to the sale

Everyone likes funny commercials. Creative people like creating them. Advertisers are pleased to be running them. The consumer enjoys them. The only problem is: people laugh at the joke and forget the product telling it.

Ban deodorant ran one of the rare humorous campaigns that also increased sales. Commercials exaggerated the problem of odor, and the solution of Ban. A man asked his psychiatrist, "If I use Ban deodorant, will it solve all my problems?" The doctor replied, "No. Just one of them."

Remember that humor wears out fast. If you run a funny campaign, you will need more commercials.

Sex: to sell sexy products

Sex may make the world go round, but it doesn't sell many products. Sex sells, if you're selling a sexy product, like perfume or cosmetics.

Weight-watching is one area where sex does work. Liquid diet products were originally sold to men on a health positioning. Sales took off when advertising told women that these diet aids could help them stay thin and sexy.

Music: to reinforce the message

Two kinds of music are common.

Songs and musical backgrounds are quick ways to evoke a mood—a sort of emotional shorthand. But use music carefully. It tends to lower the ability to recall your commercial.

Jingles, on the other hand, can increase memorability. These short, catchy tunes repeat the product name and promise, and tend to stick in the mind. They are often effective in selling products to children.

Eccentric casting: to help you stand out in the crowd

Look for actors with some quality that sets them

apart. When you cast a "typical suburban housewife," you won't offend anyone. But your commercial may be ignored.

Using a semi-celebrity in commercials often helps you stand out. Even if the consumer doesn't know his name, his face will look familiar.

Emotion: to involve the viewer

You can't *bore* a customer into buying your product. Don't be afraid of warmth. Look for a human quality in your commercial.

> *Emotional commercials for Final Touch fabric softener show husbands praising their wives for putting "so much love into everything." That campaign doubled Final Touch sales.*

Unusual film techniques: to drive home your message

Avoid using film tricks for the sake of the technique itself. That will blur your sales message. Use of an unusual technique, such as a split screen or slow motion, can be effective if it helps your commercial make its point.

Ask for an explanation, and even filmed examples, of any new or unusual film technique. Then decide if it helps. Or hurts.

* * * * *

How do you know it's a good commercial?

Look for a big idea. A storyboard that lets the picture tell the story. A simple, single-minded commercial that can be summed up in one key visual.

Is the dramatic technique appropriate to your

27

product—a demonstration of a product advantage, a believable testimonial, a relevant presenter, an involving slice?

You may like the storyboard, you may not. That's subjective. Your decision should be based on just two questions. Is it appropriate? Will it be effective?

Merrill Lynch is bullish on America.

The key visual is one frame that summarizes the entire commercial.

"You are about to witness a crime!" An attention-grabbing opening for American Express Travelers Cheques commercials.

Demonstrations don't have to be dull. International Paper drove a truck over a bridge made of paperboard.

Pete the butcher is a memorable, authoritative spokesman for Shake 'n Bake coating mix.

Chapter III

What Works Best in Print

ADVERTISERS typically ask for many more changes on a magazine layout than they do on a television storyboard. Apparently, they're held back by the technicalities of film production. But a print advertisement just sits there, unmoving and vulnerable. Print advertising is apparently so easy to do, many people can consider themselves experts. But be warned. It's only *apparently* easy.

In looking at a magazine or newspaper layout, *react first to the overall message*—the headline and illustration. Read the body copy for clarity and fact, but resist the temptation to play author. Changes in body copy cannot affect the thrust of the advertisement.

Newspaper and magazine advertisements, just like television commercials, *must* carry out the agreed-upon strategy. And, if you are supporting a television campaign with print as a secondary medium, that advertising should carry out the same theme as the television commercials.

22 Ways to Get More Effective Print Advertising

1. Get your message in the headline.

The headline should tell the whole story—including the brand name and key consumer promise. Avoid blind headlines that tell the reader nothing.

Research shows that four out of five readers do not get further than the headline. If you depend on the body copy to tell your story, *you are wasting 80 percent of your money!*

2. Use the headline to flag your prospect.

Select your audience by appealing to a reader's self-interest. If the advertising is talking to a special group, single out that prospect in the headline.

> *"Great news for mothers of cavity-prone children" was the introductory headline for Aim toothpaste.*

3. Offer a benefit in the headline.

Headlines that promise a benefit sell more than those that don't.

The *Reader's Digest*, which employs some of the best headline writers in the business, has three guiding principles for headlines. Present a benefit to the reader. Make the benefit quickly apparent. Make the benefit easy to get.

> *Among the most popular Digest subjects are money and health. "How to Cut Your Phone Bill." "Better Ways to Stop Smoking."*

4. Inject news in your headline.

Your product will be new only once. If you have a

new product, or an improvement of an existing product, announce it with a loud bang.

> *"Revolutionary new drain cleaner invented.*
> *Opens clogged drains in one second!" That*
> *headline announced new Drain Power with a*
> *bang.*

The consumer is always on the lookout for new ways to use an existing product. Ideas for new usage in your headline add news value to an old product.

5. Don't be afraid of long headlines.

Research shows that, on the average, long headlines sell more merchandise than short ones.

> *Fact-filled headlines for Toro lawn mowers run*
> *as long as 20 words. This advertising increased*
> *Toro sales by 20 percent.*

6. Avoid negative headlines.

People are literal-minded, and may remember only the negatives. Sell the positive benefits in your product—not that it won't harm, or that some defect has been solved. Look for emotional words that attract and motivate, like *free* and *new* and *love*.

7. Look for story appeal in your illustration.

Next to the headline, an illustration is the most effective way to get a reader's attention. Try for story appeal—the kind of illustration that makes the reader ask: "What's going on here?"

> *The man with the eyepatch added class and*
> *mystery to Hathaway shirt advertising. The*
> *campaign ran successfully for 20 years.*

8. Photographs are better than drawings.

Research says that photography increases recall an average of 26 percent over artwork.

> *In travel advertising, show photographs of the natives, not the tourists. KLM Royal Dutch Airlines once showed a photograph of 86 natives of Amsterdam. Research ranked it among the best-read advertisements of the year.*

9. Before-and-after photographs make a point better than words.

If you can, show a visual contrast—a change in the consumer, or a demonstration of product superiority.

> *Owens-Corning contrasts the advantages of fiber glass over traditional materials. Two illustrations are labeled "The Old Way" and "The Fiberglas Way." These advertisements are consistently among the ten best-read in The Wall Street Journal.*

10. Use simple layouts.

One big picture works better than several small pictures. Avoid cluttered pages. (Layouts that resemble the magazine's editorial format are well-read.)

11. Always put a caption under a photograph.

Readership of picture captions is generally twice as great as body copy. The picture-caption can be an advertisement by itself.

12. Don't be afraid of long copy.

The people who read beyond the headline are *prospects for your product or your service.* If your product is expensive—like a car, a vacation, or an industrial product—prospects are hungry for the information long copy gives them.

> *Advertisements for the Cessna Citation business jet use between 1,500 and 2,000 words of body copy. After one year, the Citation was outselling every other business aircraft—at three-quarters of a million dollars per sale.*

Consider long copy if you have a complex story to tell, many different product points to make, or an expensive product or service to sell.

13. Don't nitpick the body copy.

Most advertisers spend too much time worrying about body copy, less on the important overall impression of the advertisement. Just make sure the copy is clear and accurate. Look for facts, not adjectives. Specifics, not generalizations.

14. Testimonials add believability.

As in television, the endorsements of real people are memorable and persuasive.

In industrial advertising, it pays to cite case histories. Buyers like to know how well your product has worked for others.

> *International Nickel reported construction of Chattanooga Gas Company's natural gas tank four months ahead of schedule. "Easy-welding 9% Nickel Steel is One Reason Why." An impressive case history, directly responsible for new business.*

15. Avoid manufacturer talk.

Bernice FitzGibbon, the great advertising manager of Gimbel's in New York, made her writers take their copy into the store and *read it* to the customers.

Look for advertising written the way people talk.

Joe DiMaggio, as spokesman for The Bowery Savings Bank, never talks in trade jargon. By the end of his first year, The Bowery's share of growth in savings bank deposits jumped over 60 percent.

16. Do not print copy in reverse type.

It may look attractive, but it reduces readership. For the same reason, don't surprint copy on the illustration of your advertisement.

For years, Save The Children Federation used reverse plate—white type on a black background. When they tested a black-on-white version, contributions increased 65 percent.

17. Look at your advertisement in its editorial environment.

Ask to see your advertisement pasted into the magazine in which it will appear. Or, for newspapers, photostated in the same tone as the newspaper page.

Beautifully mounted layouts are deceptive. The reader will never see your advertisement printed on high-gloss paper, with a big white border, mounted on a board. It is *misleading* for you to look at it this way.

18. Develop a single advertising format.

An overall format for all print advertising can double recognition. This rule holds special meaning for industrial advertisers. One format will help readers see your advertisements as coming from one large corporation, rather than several small companies.

19. In promotion advertising, sell the promotion first.

Promotion advertising is one time your product can come second. When you offer a free steak knife (or a coupon), feature it in the headline.

20. Use conventional coupons in conventional positions.

A *Reader's Digest* analysis shows the most successful promotion advertisements contain a strong offer, and use coupons that *look* like coupons. Generally, an advertiser will request a right-hand page position, and place the coupon in the lower right-hand corner, where the reader can most easily tear it out.

21. In corporate advertising, offer service.

Corporate advertising lacks the retail discipline of selling a product. Too much is written from the corporation's interest—not the reader's. A change in corporate name, logotype, or diversification philosophy is not in itself interesting.

> *Advertising for Puerto Rico changed the image of a country. One advertisement offered tax advice by economist Beardsley Ruml; coupons were clipped by 14,000 readers, many of whom later established factories on the island.*

Good corporate advertising should answer *three* questions the reader might ask. What are they saying? Why are they saying it to me? What do they want me to do about it?

22. Make each advertisement a complete sale.

Only the advertiser reads all his advertisements. Any advertisement in a series must stand on its own. *Ev-*

ery one must make a complete sale. Assume it will be the *only* advertisement for your product a reader will ever see.

* * * * *

You can forget all these rules—*except the first one*—and still run successful print advertising. You must get your message in the headline. React to the overall impression, just as the reader will. The tendency, remember, is to turn the page. What does your advertisement offer that will *stop* someone?

A newsy headline for a new product.

Photographic contrast makes this a well-read campaign.

Long copy helped make Citation the largest-selling business aircraft.

Chapter IV

What Works Best in Radio

THE OMINOUS CREAKING of a door being opened slow-ly. That sound produced weekly chills among the radio audience for "The Inner Sanctum." It was partic-ularly effective if you listened in the dark.

Mystery programs like "The Inner Sanctum" characterized the 1940s. Sounds like the creaking door produced visual effects beyond the reach of television.

The unique strength of radio is *its power to stir the imagination.*

> *"Okay people, now when I give the cue, I want the 700-foot mountain of whipped cream to roll into Lake Michigan, which has been drained and filled with hot chocolate. Then the Royal Canadian Air Force will fly overhead towing a ten-ton maraschino cherry which will be dropped into the whipped cream, to the cheering of 25,000 extras." Comedian Stan Freberg created that commercial to demonstrate the unique power of radio to stretch the imagination.*

There are more radios than people in the United States today; more than 400 million sets in homes, in cars, on the beaches. Since almost everyone has a radio, people tend to listen alone. And they choose exactly the kind of

40

program they want to hear—news, rock, talk, classical or sports.

That audience segmentation is a great advantage to advertisers. *Radio lets you select your audience.*

Finally, it is the most *flexible* medium. You can get on (or off) the air quickly. You can change your message at the last minute. You can schedule your advertising according to the season, the weather or the time of day.

Imagination. Selectivity. Flexibility.

What are the other special characteristics of radio?

It is a very *personal* medium. You can talk directly to the listener, and be very involving—once you get his (or her) attention.

There's a lot of *competition.* The average station plays 15 or more commercials an hour (although the trend is down).

Be intrusive!

Radio is like television in some important respects. It shares the same dramatic techniques—slice-of-life, testimonial, presenter, and music. And, like any other good advertising, is based on sound positioning and a meaningful consumer benefit.

How to Get Better Radio Commercials

1. Stretch the listener's imagination.

Voices and sounds can evoke pictures.

Josiah S. Carberry, the world's most traveled man, is found on top of a pyramid, on a ship in Acapulco Bay, at a Hawaiian luau. Radio

commercials for American Express Travel
Service use sound and imagery to take
Carberry—and the listener—all over the globe.

2. Listen for a memorable sound.

What will make your commercial stand out from the clutter? A distinctive voice, a memorable jingle, a solution to the listener's problem.

Pepperidge Farm radio advertising stands out
because of the distinctive Yankee twang of its
spokesman, Titus Moody.

3. Present one idea.

It is difficult to communicate more than one idea in a television commercial. In radio, which is subject to more distractions, it is nearly impossible. Be direct and clear.

Retail stores are heavy users of radio. While they
often sell several products at a time, the best
commercials sell a single idea—like a storewide
sale.

4. Select your audience quickly.

It pays to flag your segment of the audience at the beginning of the commercial—before they can switch to another station.

Hay-fever commercials for Contac capsules were
run only on days when the pollen count was above
certain minimum levels. Live announcements of
the local pollen count preceded each commercial.

5. Mention your brand name and your promise early.

Commercials that do so get higher awareness. It

heightens awareness if you mention the brand name
and promise *more than once*.

6. Capitalize on events.

Exploit the flexibility of radio to tie in with fads,
fashions, news events, or the weather.

Sears ordered special radio commercials during
snowstorms to announce that their stores would
stay open late to sell snow tires.

7. Use radio to reach teenagers.

Teenagers don't watch much television. They do
listen to a lot of radio. Media experts say it's the best way
to reach teens. Some say it's the *only* way.

Bruce Morrow ("Cousin Brucie"), the leading
disc jockey on a big New York contemporary
station, really understands his audience. He says
one of the most successful campaigns on his
station told young listeners about a line of shoes:
"Your father would never wear them."

8. Music can help.

It is particularly effective in reaching teenagers,
who prefer the "now sounds" offered by music stations.
You can give your campaign infinite variety with the
same lyrics arranged in different ways, and sung by different people.

Great Shakes shake mix used "Top 40" singers
and groups to create many different sounds for the
same set of lyrics: "Anyplace can be a soda
fountain now, with Great Shakes. New Great
Shakes."

9. Keep the music simple.

Use jingles or simple lyrics that repeat your brand name and promise over and over. Research shows that complex music and sophisticated lyrics get low recall scores.

Many years after it had stopped running, women were still able to play back, word for word, a simple radio jingle: "Rinso White, Rinso bright, Happy little washday song."

Don't let the music overpower the words—and your message.

10. Drivers are a relatively attentive audience.

Research says that drivers recall the commercial message better than home listeners. Don't neglect radio if you are selling gasoline, tires, mufflers—anything to do with cars and driving.

The sounds of screeching tires and honking horns dramatized the dangers of driving while drowsy. This NoDoz commercial urged drivers to keep a packet handy in the glove compartment.

11. Ask listeners to take action.

People respond to radio requests for action. They call the station to exchange views with the disc jockey, or ask for certain music. Don't be afraid to ask listeners to call now, or write in, or send money.

The familiar notes of Beethoven's Fifth Symphony are stopped in full blast. "We stopped the music to start you thinking" began the fund-raising message for The New York Philharmonic. "Don't let the music stop"

44

*appealed successfully to music lovers listening to
their radios. The Philharmonic closed the gap in
its deficit.*

12. Use the strength of radio personalities.

Consider commercials delivered live instead of recorded ones. Many of the local station disc jockeys and
personalities have a strong hold on their audiences. If
they believe in your product, they can sell it better than
you can.

*Capitalize on the announcer's own style. Send a
sample of your product, and a fact sheet.
Enthusiasm adds a dimension to an improvised
commercial.*

13. Have enough commercials in your pool.

Radio is a high-frequency medium. You need
more commercials in your campaign than you do with
television. You also must refresh your pool with new
commercials more often. *Humorous commercials fare the
worst with repetition.*

14. Reach ethnic groups with special messages.

There are many Black and foreign language stations. It pays to create radio advertising designed for
ethnic groups. A translation of your basic campaign *may*
be effective; a special message developed for a special
audience may do even better.

15. "Prime Time" offers special benefits.

Understand that radio's prime time is 6 A.M. to 10
A.M. It's a unique opportunity to remind people about
breakfast products—coffee, cereal, orange juice.

16. Use radio for special promotions.

A sale at the local department store. A feature at the corner movie house. Radio lends itself to "this week only" promotions.

Summer is off-season for Puerto Rico. But its tourist bureau went on radio to invite travelers to take advantage of special "Summer Trade Wind" rates. Bookings rose over previous years.

17. Use "imagery transfer."

Transfer sound elements of your television campaign over to radio. Listeners will be reminded of the film they saw and can often play back the action of the television commercial scene for scene. (In rare instances, you can simply lift the entire audio track and turn it into a radio spot.) Image transfer is a way to add frequency and awareness to a television campaign.

18. Don't ever look at a commercial in script form.

If listeners miss a part of your message, they can't go back and read it again. The copywriter should *read* a radio commercial to you. Or you can ask to hear a rough approximation of the finished commercial.

19. Judge your radio commercials in context.

Just as you ask to see your print advertisement pasted into a magazine, ask to hear the radio commercial spliced into a tape of several minutes of actual program content.

Listen to the commercial on something other than the most expensive hi-fi loudspeaker, and closer to the quality of a six-transistor portable.

Production of Radio Commercials

Radio is the easiest production process to understand. It is usually the quickest and the least expensive.

The simplest form of radio is live delivery. The agency provides a script to be delivered by the station's own announcer. It must be accurately timed for length.

Recorded commercials are usually produced on audio tape. It's similar to home-recording tape, except that the quality is better.

Your first step in tape production is hearing audition tapes of the recommended talent—announcers, music groups, etc. You may sometimes hear a *demo* tape (or *scratch track*) that suggests the finished commercial, minus rehearsals and polishing.

The next step is the recording session. The entire commercial may be recorded in one piece, or individual elements recorded separately. Voices and music, for example, are put on separate tapes and then mixed.

Duplicates of the final, approved commercial are called *dubs*.

* * * * *

Select your audience by station, time of day, season of the year. Rely on radio's flexibility to keep your message current. Above all, stretch the listener's imagination. Television limits you to the 21-inch screen. Radio sets no limits at all.

Radio reaches drivers. Commercials dramatize the dangers of driving while drowsy, suggested keeping NoDoz handy in the glove compartment.

Radio flexibility. Contac used pollen count reports to reach hay fever sufferers. The higher the pollen count, the more commercials.

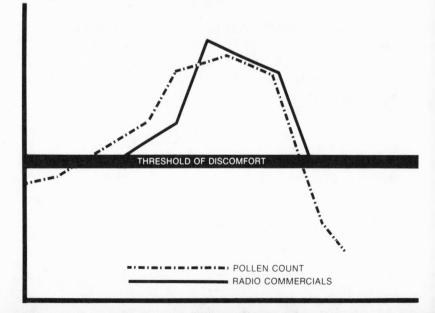

THRESHOLD OF DISCOMFORT

POLLEN COUNT
RADIO COMMERCIALS

Chapter V

What Works Best in Outdoor and Transit

A￼LL OUTDOOR ADVERTISING, from a giant highway poster to a child's lemonade stand, has one thing in common. *It sells to an audience in motion.*

The consumer is *moving past* your advertising, and you have only seconds to communicate your entire message—the experts say no more than *ten* seconds.

People driving past your poster can't stop for a second look, even if they want to. You don't have time for more than one big simple idea.

Transit advertising inside buses and subways is just the opposite; it gives you time to deliver your message. These travelers are a *captive audience.* They often have little else to distract them. And the average ride is *22.7 minutes* (says the Transit Advertising Association).

This chapter will give you some tips on how to cope with both audiences.

What Works Best in Outdoor

Outdoor has enormous *impact*, because it is so much larger than life. It follows that your billboard concept should be larger than life, too. Great size only magnifies dullness.

How to flash your message—fast—to a moving audience. That's the challenge. Outdoor works like a 10-second TV commercial—it is basically *reminder* advertising, and can deliver a message with great frequency.

Although outdoor is often used by banks and cars (which would benefit from longer copy), it is underused by food and toiletry products (which are bought more frequently).

Another advantage of outdoor is the ability to zero in on a target. It is *the most localized* of all media. You can select an audience with precision. And reach the consumer, outside the house, often on the way to buy.

Here are 13 guidelines for looking at outdoor:

1. Look for a big idea.

This is no place for subtleties. Outdoor is a bold medium. You need a poster that registers the idea quickly and memorably. A "visual scandal" that shocks the viewer into awareness.

> *Open Pit barbecue sauce sells its "outdoor" flavor with a startling illustration of the bottle being skewered on a barbecue fork. This campaign increased awareness nearly four times in test market.*

2. Keep it simple.

Cut out all extraneous words and pictures, and concentrate on the essentials. Outdoor is the art of brevity. Use only one picture, and no more than seven words of copy—preferably less.

3. Use bold lettering.

Avoid special typefaces, like scripts. To be readable at 100 feet, letters must be at least three inches high. To be readable at 400 feet, at least one-foot letters are needed.

4. Use art for impact.

Foster & Kleiser, one of the biggest outdoor companies, advises the use of strong silhouettes—and photographs cropped and enlarged to "heroic proportions." Outdoor is great for appetite appeal.

5. Use color for readability.

The most readable combination is black on yellow. Other combinations may gain more attention, but stay with primary colors—and *stay away from reverse.*

Fluorescent colors also increase impact and visibility. But use with care: they can create a circus effect.

6. Use the location to your advantage.

Many new housing developments capitalize on their convenient locations with a poster saying: "If you lived here, you'd be home now." Use outdoor to tell drivers that your restaurant is down the road, your department store is across the street.

Don't ignore the ability of outdoor to reach ethnic neighborhoods. Tailor the language and the models to your consumer.

7. Look for human, emotional content for memorability.

Outdoor is one medium where humor may work.

It can be an entertainment medium for travelers who are hungry or bored.

Burma-Shave was an early outdoor advertiser.
Its sequential signs on the sides of roads in the
1930s were memorized by travelers: "Riot in the
drugstore . . . calling all cars . . . 100
customers, 99 jars . . . Burma-Shave."

8. Announce new products with an extra bang.

You can reach 45 percent of households *in the first day*, according to Nielsen. Use outdoor for *quick* reach and extra impact.

Outdoor posters announced the arrival of Maxim
with a giant jar and the simple message:
"Freeze-dried coffee is here!"

Don't overlook the impact on the *trade*. The local supermarket manager may never see your commercials on daytime television. He will notice your advertising if there's a big outdoor poster across the street from his store.

9. Remind people about your television campaign.

What is the *key visual* of your television campaign? Think about turning it into an outdoor poster.

Nationwide Insurance uses the same blanket
always featured in television commercials—the
symbol of their "blanket coverage."

10. Use the flexibility of outdoor.

You can buy a citywide posting, a center-city or neighborhood posting, a supermarket posting, or a single panel. The standard term to describe the exposure of an outdoor posting used to be a *showing*. The industry is now converting to broadcast terminology.

A #100 "showing" is the same as 100 gross rating points. (See the chapter on media.) It means enough posters to be seen daily by people equivalent to the total population in a market.

11. Personalize when you can.

Personalized posters are practical, even for short runs. Mention a specific geographical area ("New in Chicago"), or the name of a local dealer.

Shell offered its dealers a choice of more than 30 different posters. Each had a space for the name of the dealer. The most popular of the monthly messages dealt with spring tune-ups and winterizing. The poster chosen least said: "I like kids. Bring your bike in for air anytime."

12. Look at the advertising in context.

Have your outdoor board reduced to a photostat about three inches high, so you get the same size impression from across your office as driving by 100 feet away.

13. Ride the showing.

You can't judge outdoor in your office or even by one board specially posted for your approval. The only way to get a feel for what works and what doesn't is to drive around a market. Then you'll see your board in rain, in shadows, partially blocked by buildings or trucks—and these rules become more believable.

What Works Best
in Transit Advertising

Transit is both interior and exterior. More advertising dollars are invested in posters on the *outside* of buses or on train platforms. The creative rules are the same as for outdoor boards.

Posters *inside* buses and subways are a unique medium. You have time to get your message across, and remarkable opportunities for frequency and repetition.

The rider averages 24 rides per month, according to the Transit Advertising Association. Workers, shoppers and students see your message over and over again.

Here are four points to consider in dealing with transit copy:

1. Think about your audience.

Transit advertising works well for beverages, foods, and "get away from it all" products, like travel. You are talking to people who may be thirsty, hungry, or tired.

"A lady on this train has a girdle that's killing her." Ammens medicated powder appealed with humor to the special problems of the transit audience.

2. Buy special routes.

Buy space on a subway route that stops beneath your department store. Or a bus that passes your theatre. Think about the destination of most of the passengers; some bus routes let you select an audience of high-income consumers.

3. Use transit to deliver a coupon.

"Take-ones"—pads of tear-off blanks pasted onto an advertisement—can deliver an application or a request for more information.

> *The Bowery Savings Bank uses "take-ones" to deliver an application blank the rider can fill out for more information on savings bank life insurance.*

4. Be imaginative.

The automobile created outdoor advertising; now the growth of mass transportation is creating new opportunities for transit. Many communities have begun to provide buses to take commuters to and from train stations. Suburban women hire a weekly bus for shopping and theatre in the city.

> *A fairly recent trend is "the basic bus"—an entire bus taken over by just one advertiser. Caution: this media buy works best when you have several important things to say, or more than one product to sell.*

A Guide to Outdoor Production

Outdoor boards are usually printed, and therefore don't represent a unique production process. (See the chapter on print production.) However, some boards in high-traffic locations are semipermanent, and the advertisement is *painted* on the board.

What makes outdoor different is the *size* of the poster. The outdoor company takes the design for the board, enlarges and projects it on master sheets, and then lays it out in ten huge sections for printing. This series of ten sheets makes up the total design.

Standard outdoor sizes refer back to the days when printing presses couldn't handle big sheets of paper. A 24-sheet poster now means a *size*—about nine feet by 20 feet—no longer the *number* of sheets. (The 30-sheet board is about ten feet by 22 feet. The *bleed* board is a 30-sheet, without a border.)

Cutouts or extensions can extend billboard areas, for a price. Overlays (called *snipes*) can add copy over an existing board—to change copy, list a local dealer, or announce a new date.

The key to keeping the costs down and getting the best reproduction is *time*.

Allow 20 working days for four-color outdoor boards, somewhat less for solid colors. Then add a week for shipping and ten days more prior to posting. (For painted boards, allow 45 days.)

(There are no special terms for transit advertising, which is also simply printing. But there is a variety of sizes in posters for the sides and ends of buses and subways, outside vehicles and stations, illuminated clocks and special station displays.)

* * * * *

With outdoor, you have only seconds to reach your mobile audience. "A poster should be to the eye what a shouted demand is to the ear," said poster artist C. B. Falls. The only shout it will hear is *one big idea.*

Look for a big idea. A startling outdoor board for barbecue sauce.

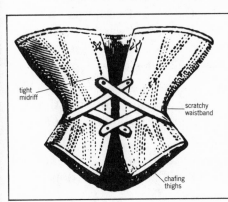

A LADY ON THIS TRAIN HAS A GIRDLE THAT'S KILLING HER. Maybe you can spot her. Every time she moves, <u>it</u> rubs. She should try Medicated Ammens Powder. It contains a dry lubricant that turns painful rub into comfortable <u>slide</u>. Absorbs moisture, too. A blessing in this weather. Good reasons to soothe, cool, refresh with Ammens today.

An appeal to the special problems of the subway rider.

Illuminated clocks are a unique transit opportunity.

Chapter VI

What Works Best in Direct Mail

"WE LEARN the principles and prove them by repeated tests. This is done through keyed advertising, by traced returns, largely by the use of coupons. We compare one way with many others, backward and forward, and record the results. When one method invariably proves best, that method becomes a fixed principle."

That was written in 1923 by Claude Hopkins, the great copywriter of Lord & Thomas. His book, *Scientific Advertising*, went on to state:

"Mail order advertising is traced down to the fraction of a penny. The cost per reply and cost per dollar of sale show up with utter exactness."

That *accountability* is one of the two special characteristics of direct mail.

The other is its *selectivity*. Direct mail is the perfect example of the rifle shot compared to the buckshot of other media.

Direct mail can sell almost any product from a packet of flower seeds to a $4,000 car.

"I am looking for 1,000 Americans who are

willing to invest in something different in the way of automobiles.

"If you are one of them, I can offer you free fuel . . . free motor oil . . . free oil filters . . . and free lubrication for the first 15,000 miles you own and drive an amazing Mercedes-Benz car.

"This is my way of introducing the Mercedes-Benz 190 Diesel to men of influence in the community."

That was the opening of a letter that resulted in sales of over $2½ million.

The *advantages* of direct mail are considerable. It is quick and flexible. It introduces new products. It reaches the best prospects. It generates sales leads. It tests prices—and advertising promises. It calls for action by the reader.

These assets lead to huge investments by advertisers. Both the money spent and the opportunities available dictate that direct mail be considered an *advertising* medium—an integral part of the marketing plan, subject to the same disciplines of strategy and execution.

What we've been talking about—direct mail—is *part* of the total *direct response* (or direct marketing) business. The other part—mail order advertising in general media (magazines, newspapers, radio and TV)—is less selective than using a mailing list. It is, however, equally accountable.

It pays to test

Endless testing—of copy, layout, color, offers, terms, prices, premiums, envelopes, mailing lists, of the total package. The secret of successful direct mail is in knowing what *has* worked, and challenging those results with *new* testing every time. Very hard work.

The basis for evaluation is *maximum cost efficiency* against a given marketing objective:

- Not just the response rate, but the *cost per inquiry* (CPI).
- Not just the quantity of response, but the *conversion rate* from inquiry to sale.

This leads to a related concept of evaluation: *the true value of a customer.* If you use only efficiency as the basis for all evaluation, you will end with the cheapest mailing packages or tiny mail order advertisements. But if you understand the value of a customer in terms of the profitability of a sale, the door opens for more expensive mailings or larger advertisements . . . so long as they are productive. The true-value concept also extends to purchases over time, if a product is one that can be bought several times over a period of several years.

Thanks to the precision of measurement in direct marketing, some general principles can be established. But, warns direct mail expert Barry Blau, *"The greatest rule of all is that there are always exceptions to every rule. Testing must be the final arbiter."*

What Works Best in Direct Response Advertising

Here are a dozen general principles:

1. Make sure your offer is right.

More than any other element, what you offer the consumer—in terms of product, price or premium—

will make the difference. Consider combinations instead of single units, optional extras, different opening offers and commitment periods.

> *The way you position your offer can double your response. Burpee changed from headlining a $1 seed offer to a free garden catalog—and improved response 112 percent.*

Free is the most powerful offer you can make, but beware of its attracting lookers instead of buyers.

2. Demonstrate your product.

Offer a free sample, or enclose a sample if you can. Sampling is the most expensive promotion in absolute cost, but is often so effective that the investment is quickly paid back with a larger business base.

> *Full-size samples generally work better than smaller trial sizes. They give people a chance to get used to a new product. Often a coupon for a full-size sample will work better than a small trial size in the mail.*

Less expensive mailings often outperform more costly ones. But if you measure response on a profit per piece mailed, it sometimes pays to spend a few more cents.

3. Use the envelope to telegraph your message.

Direct mail must work fast. Your envelope has only seconds to interest the prospect, or go unopened into the wastebasket.

> *"Four contemporary American plays for $25 total—excellent seats for lively productions at what Clive Barnes calls 'one of those rare theatres where everything seems right.'*
>
> *"What's the catch? See inside."*

Subscriptions increased 50 percent when The American Place Theatre changed to a new brochure with this provocative cover.

4. Have a copy strategy.

Like any other advertising medium, direct mail will be more productive if you decide *in advance* the important issues of target audience, consumer benefit and support, tone and personality.

While your promise should relate specifically to your product, experts say the most potent appeals in direct mail are how to make money, save money, save time, or avoid effort.

5. Grab the reader's attention.

Every beginning copywriter in direct mail learns the AIDA formula. The letters stand for the ideal structure of a sales letter: Attention, Interest, Desire, Action. Look for a dramatic opening, one that speaks to the reader in a very *personal* way.

> *"When this train emerges from the tunnel at 108th Street this evening, look out of the window.*
>
> *"You may see some of the 1,125 boys and girls from New York ghettos who are now on vacation from our Negro colleges."*
>
> *This was the opening of a letter to commuters on their way home through Harlem. It was for the United Negro College Fund.*

6. Don't be afraid of long copy.

The more you tell, the more you sell—particularly if you're asking the reader to spend much money or invest time. The Mercedes-Benz Diesel car letter was five pages long. A Cunard Line letter for ocean cruises was eight pages long.

The key to long copy is *facts.* Be specific, not general. Make the letter visually appealing. Break up the copy into smaller paragraphs and emphasize important points with underlines or handwritten notes. Including several pieces in a direct mail package often improves response.

> *Time-Life Records promoted a Tchaikovsky series with a letter, record, brochure, and response card. Response was increased with a fifth enclosure—a letter "from the composer," drawn from his writings.*

7. Don't let the reader off the hook.

Leave your readers with something to do, so that they won't procrastinate. It's too easy to put off a decision. Use action devices like a yes/no token to be stuck on a reply card. *Involvement* is important.

Prod them to act *now.* Set a fixed period of time, like 10 days. Or make only a limited supply available. Make it extremely easy for the reader to respond to your offer. But always ask for the order.

8. Pretest your promises and headlines.

Don't guess at what will appeal to the reader. There are many ways to sell your product benefits, and as many inexpensive testing methods.

> *Headlines can be tested in small-space newspaper advertisements. Another interesting device is to use envelopes to test different copy appeals.*

Avoid humor, tricks or gimmicks. It pays to be serious and helpful.

9. Make your catalog work hard.

Every product offered should be measured in terms of profit per square inch of page space. Cut out the weak products, or at least give them less room. (Small-space newspaper or magazine insertions can be used to test new products versus proven ones.)

Put your winners up-front in the catalog. They will get attention, and hold readers.

10. Give something away.

Premiums almost always build response. They need not be expensive; often good premiums can be created from materials on hand (brochures, etc.). But test your premiums to make sure you have the most appealing ones to offer. They need not be related to the product.

11. Test, test, test.

Test your product, price, and premium. All these often have more influence on the outcome than the copy itself. Test size, position, color versus black-and-white. Sometimes color pays, sometimes not.

Test your media and mailing lists. Try anything that seems reasonable, but don't commit to broad-scale mailings until you are *sure* they will be profitable. (Wait to see final sales results before mailing an entire list based on successful initial response.)

12. Repeat your winners.

A profitable product should be tested in new media and larger space. Mailings should be expanded. New lists tested.

Repeat your profitable mailings to the same lists. It often pays.

Resist the need to change for change's sake.

*One advertisement ran almost unchanged for 40
years with the headline "Do you make these
mistakes in English?" It was a mail order
advertisement for the Sherwin Cody School of
English, which could measure the results.*

* * * * *

Rising costs of paper and postage put special pressures on direct mail. But these are more than outweighed by fundamental trends that favor the special strengths of direct response advertising.

The major new advertising need is for media to reach special audience *segments.* Selectivity is the strength of direct response.

Mailing lists have always been selective. Now computers use "merge-purge" programs to combine lists and eliminate duplication. Lists built on ZIP code analyses select audiences on the basis of geography or demographic characteristics. Criteria grids help build mailing lists of high potential prospects based on age, income, profession, family status, car ownership, location, and similar characteristics.

Direct marketing is increasingly becoming a *convenience.* Shopping by mail (or telephone) is encouraged by the increase in working women and by the availability of credit cards. A dramatic example of this trend is the fact that record promotions are now among the largest advertisers on spot television.

But most of all, direct mail is an *accountable* medium. Advertising, said Claude Hopkins, "is not for general effect. It is not to keep your name before the people. Treat it as a salesman. Force it to justify itself. Compare it with other salesmen. Figure its cost and result."

Burpee's New 1975 Garden Catalog-Free

Grow Your Own Delicious Vegetables and Save Money

Gardening is a wonderful experience for the whole family. And today, growing your own delicious vegetables could save you hundreds of dollars.

These outstanding selections are just a few of the dozens of exciting varieties and new hybrids in the Burpee 1975 Garden Catalog along with over 1,400 other vegetables, flowers, fruits, shrubs, trees, and garden aids.

The new 164-page Burpee Garden Catalog is yours free. It is a comprehensive planting and growing guide with 600 photos—450 in color—and many helpful hints. You get expert advice on how to get the most for your gardening dollar with high-yield vegetables.

Since 1876, Burpee has been developing new vegetable varieties that are easier to grow and produce more bountiful yields in less space, as well as new and better flowers. As a result, Burpee is America's leading breeder of flowers and vegetables for the home gardener. Many new varieties and famous favorites are available only from Burpee.

Join the millions of home gardeners who benefit from the horticultural advice in the Burpee Garden Catalog. Send for your free copy today.

1. Burpee's Ambrosia Hybrid Cantaloupe—"Food for the gods"—we said when we tasted this mouth-watering new cantaloupe. So we called it Ambrosia. A product of 10 years of research and cross-

research, the sturdy vines produce bumper crops of 4½ to 5 lb. melons, with extremely small seed cavities and thick, juicy flesh edible right to the thin rind. Just 86 days from seed to delicious fruit.

2. Early Girl Tomato—A new hybrid that matures very early, in beautiful clusters on wilt-resistant plants, and continues producing longer than most early types. Glossy, very smooth, blemish-free fruits, average 4-5 oz., with bright scarlet meaty interiors. Excellent flavor. Table-ripe in 54 days.

3. Burpee Hybrid Zucchini Squash—Ideal for small gardens as these bush-like, compact plants thrive in limited space. Ripens early and gives heavy yield over a long period of time. Ready in about 50 days after planting.

4. Green Ice Lettuce—A Burpee triumph for the home garden! 10 years of research and cross-

breeding to develop. The first vegetable variety to be "patented." Delicious, easy-to-grow, and vigorous. Matures in 45 days and produces longer because it is so slow to go to seed. *Available only from Burpee.* U.S. Plant Var. Cert. #7100001.

5. Roma Bush Bean®—Great for small gardens. Plants need very little space and grow without support, giving generous crops of long, wide-podded beans. Exceptionally tender and meaty. Excellent for freezing. Ready to pick in 53 days.

6. Candy Cane Zinnias—Triumph of the flower-breeder's art that took 15 years to develop. A spectacular new zinnia striped pink, rose, or cerise on white background, like Christmas candy. Some bloom yellow-gold with flecked orange-scarlet stripes. Beautiful 3½" to 4½" flowers bloom midsummer to frost.

® Denotes that protection has been applied for under the U.S. Plant Variety Protection Act.

BURPEE'S $1 SPRING SPECIAL INTRODUCTORY OFFER

Get All Five Kinds of Easy-to-Grow Favorite Seeds—$2.75 VALUE—for only... **$1**

W. ATLEE BURPEE COMPANY
2505 Burpee Building, Warminster, Pennsylvania 18974

☐ Send FREE Burpee 1975 Catalog postpaid. (If you ordered from Burpee in 1974, your new catalog will be sent to you.)

☐ Send ___ set(s) of the 5 Favorite Seeds Special @ $1 per set. Enclosed is $ ___

NAME _____
(PLEASE PRINT)

ADDRESS _____

CITY _____ STATE _____ ZIP _____

1. **Giant Ruffled Snapdragons**—Bright colors. 2½-foot spikes. Reg. 50¢ pkt. 2. **Crown Jewels Petunias**—Mixed colors. Bloom all season. Reg. 50¢ pkt. 3. **Magic Carpet® Double Portulaca**—Mixed colors bloom all season on creeping sun-loving plants. Reg. 50¢ pkt. 4. **Alaska Giant Marigolds**—Almost white. Blooms on 2-foot plants. Reg. 50¢ pkt. 5. **Burpeeana Giant Zinnias**—5"-to-6" early blooms. All colors. Reg. 75¢ pkt.

Burpee's best catalog ever—with seeds, shrubs, trees, gardening information and everything for your garden.

Make sure your offer is right. Burpee moved its catalog offer into the headline and improved response 112 percent.

The American Place Theatre

ELEVENTH SEASON

111 West 46th Street, New York, N.Y. 10036 (212) 247-0393

Four contemporary American plays for $25 total—excellent seats for lively productions at what Clive Barnes calls "one of those rare theatres where everything seems right."

What's the catch? See inside.

The American Place Theatre is now in its new building at 46th Street and Sixth Avenue. *"This creation in the basement of a skyscraper is a great theatre,"* says Clive Barnes.

Use your envelope. Subscriptions increased 50 percent when The American Place Theatre changed to a new brochure with this provocative cover.

Include several pieces in a mailing. Response to a Time-Life Records offer increased with five enclosures in a Tchaikovsky mailing.

Chapter VII

The Why and How of Campaigns

A SINGLE ADVERTISEMENT can be memorable and persuasive. But it usually takes a campaign—*a series of different advertisements with a single goal*—to win the battle for a place in the consumer's mind.

Perhaps you aren't convinced you need a campaign at all. We're going to give you several good reasons why an advertising *campaign* works harder than unrelated one-shots, and a checklist to help you decide whether any advertisement you look at could be the start of a long-term campaign idea. You'll read a case history of the careful building of a famous campaign. And get some thoughts on campaign wear-out.

Why a Campaign Makes Advertising Work Harder

Campaigns keep creative work on target.

The agency doesn't have to consider, and test, dozens of new ideas every time a new advertisement needs to be produced. Nor does the advertiser. A campaign allows creative people to concentrate on new and better ways to communicate the same idea.

Every Zippo lighter advertisement told how a Zippo stood up under a real-life torture test. The campaign was backed by the promise "It works—or we fix it . . . free." Zippo became the best-known lighter in America and a synonym for reliability.

Campaigns are dollar-stretchers.

When consumers become familiar with your message, they do a lot of the work for you. They'll read the extra thoughts from a 60-second commercial into a 30-second one—even though you don't include them.

People pay more attention to advertising they know. It's like seeing a familiar face that stands out in a crowd.

The smaller your advertising budget, the more important it is to have a campaign.

Is It a Campaign? Four Checkpoints

When you look at one rough layout, or one television storyboard, how do you know whether or not it's a potential campaign? If the prototype advertisement is a big idea, it usually points the way quickly and clearly to future executions.

When you consider a new campaign idea, ask the agency to outline other executions: a few paragraphs describing future commercials, a few headlines indicating future print advertisements.

The essential ingredient of a campaign is *similarity* between one advertisement and another. No campaign has to pass all the following tests—although many of them do. It must pass at least *one* of them.

1. Visual similarity

This type of continuity can be established in many ways. One is using the *same spokesman*: either an invented character (Pete the butcher for Shake 'n Bake) or a real person (an actress or sports figure). It can even be an animated spokesman (Big Fig for Fig Newtons cakes).

A *demonstration* that never varies gives you similarity. Contac's tiny time pills. The cleansing cream pouring into Dove beauty bar.

> *The car that hurtled through a paper barrier was for years a demonstration of Shell gasoline performance. This campaign helped move Shell from sixth place to second in gasoline sales.*

Another visual link is the *mnemonic device*—like the crown that popped on people's heads to symbolize the "fit for a king" flavor of Imperial margarine.

The visual style or "feel" of each advertisement contributes to a campaign. In newspapers and magazines, it pays to stick with one format, one typeface that helps develop continuity. Check your newspapers and see if you can identify the retail advertisers—without seeing the name of the store.

2. Verbal similarity

This is most often a memorable set of *words* that sums up the benefit of your product or service. (Pepperidge Farm products have old-fashioned goodness because "Pepperidge Farm Remembers.") A catchy phrase alone will not give you a good campaign. You must find a word or a phrase that is consistent with your positioning and your brand personality. It should illuminate your advertising.

> *"Nationwide is on your side" is more than a rhyme. It sets the attitude for advertisements that show this insurance company cares about the human needs of its clients.*

3. A similarity of sound

A distinctive *sound* can build a campaign for radio or television commercials.

> *One of the most familiar sounds on television is the chiming doorbell that means "Avon Calling."*

The musical percolator was a memorable sound that advertised Maxwell House coffee.

A unique *voice* is a theme sound that also helps carry a campaign over into radio advertising.

A *song* can create a campaign. It can be the main element of the commercial or simply a musical tag (Campbell Soup's 30-year old "Mmm-mmm-good").

4. Similarity of attitude

In this type of campaign, the advertising expresses a distinct and consistent attitude toward the product and the people who use it.

> *The people who run Baskin-Robbins say, "We don't sell ice cream. We sell fun." The attitude is expressed in the funny, irreverent flavor names (Baseball Nut, Here Comes The Fudge), and in the cartoon-type advertising. It has helped build Baskin-Robbins from three stores in 1946 to an international chain of over 1,500 stores.*

The attitude of your campaign is really an expression of your brand personality. Few great campaigns have ever been built on this element *alone*. However, a consistent attitude is the extra ingredient that makes great campaigns great.

How To Build a Campaign: A Case History

A Mercedes-Benz barrels down the hairpin curves of a mountain, or clings impossibly to the vertical wall of a test track at more than 90 mph. A familiar sight on television. Most newspaper readers recognize the fact-filled long-copy advertisements.

Since the founding of Mercedes-Benz of North America in 1965, *one advertising campaign* has helped it achieve an 80 percent share of the $10,000-and-over car market.

Yet the idea for the campaign did not spring full-grown from a copywriter's head. It grew.

First, the positioning. "We positioned the Mercedes-Benz instantly—and on judgment—as a performance car," says a copywriter who worked on the original advertisements. "It had to be *driven* to be understood. Research confirmed our decision."

More research defined the target audience. Mercedes-Benz buyers are in the same high-income bracket as Cadillac buyers; but their *attitudes* are very different. One attitude research study termed them "the sensible rich."

The creative group developed a personality profile of the Mercedes-Benz as a guide to future executions.

"Every car is a compromise. It must strike a balance between the desirable and the possible. So automotive designers must delicately juggle all these factors, trying to score as high as possible in every area without giving up too much in any other area.

"How well does Mercedes-Benz score?

"The Mercedes-Benz loses less often than any other car. It is the most perfectly balanced car in the world."

A strategy was agreed upon. Mercedes-Benz advertising must demonstrate the car's vast range of abilities, showing *how it works* and *what makes it work*.

With less than one million dollars to spend in the first year, Mercedes-Benz decided to concentrate on newspapers.

Early advertisements ran to more than 1,000 words and included a coupon. The copy talked about engineering, safety, and performance. The company received thousands of requests for brochures.

Print advertising has remained the basic medium for Mercedes-Benz advertising. People who pay $10,000 for a car want to know a lot of details. The Mercedes-Benz customer, in particular, is a knowledgeable car buff. Long copy is the only way to tell the *complete performance story*.

Television, on the other hand, is the medium best suited to *show performance*. The most effective commercials proved to be torture-test demonstrations.

A Mercedes-Benz swerves suddenly to avoid a truck, swerves again to miss an oncoming car in the same lane by no more than one foot. This

hair-raising demonstration of maneuverability
was named the world's best live-action
commercial in 1969.

Mercedes-Benz used other media to special advantage. Magazines, to show the car in color. Radio, localized with the name and address of a dealer. Direct mail, to select high-income prospects.

No matter what the medium, the advertising campaign was the same. The visual similarity, the consistent attitude are summed up in the promise:

Mercedes-Benz—engineered like no other car in
the world.

Adding News to An Existing Campaign

Product-improvement time can be a dangerous time for a campaign. Agencies and advertisers often feel—wrongly—that a new campaign is needed to announce the improvement.

Unless your product improvement results in a change of strategy that can't be handled by your current campaign, it pays to stick with advertising that is working for you.

Commander Whitehead successfully launched
Schweppes Bitter Lemon with the same strategy
used for Tonic Water: an adult, sophisticated
premium product . . . with
"Schweppervescence."

Advertisers often put extra spending behind product improvement announcements. If you throw away a successful campaign, you throw away money already invested. Isn't it better to use those extra dollars to develop awareness of your product improvement—instead of awareness of your new campaign?

The Backup Campaign

While your current campaign is running successfully, you will want your agency to look for ways to strengthen it.

At the same time, you should think about what you are going to do *next*. You may want to test advertising for a completely new campaign. But don't be lulled into a false sense of security just because you have a backup campaign that tested well.

The market situation changes continually. You are not standing still; neither is your competition. The way people talk and dress and even think changes from year to year. Advertising that was written only 12 months ago can smack of old age today. Creative development is a continuing project.

The danger of a backup campaign is that it takes your eye off the ball—improving the *current* advertising.

If your existing campaign isn't effective, get a new one. But if it *is* working, spend as much time refining your current campaign as in looking for alternatives.

* * * * *

How long should you stay with one campaign? It's too glib to answer: "As long as it's working." Too many brands have experienced a sales problem, switched campaigns to cure it, and found they were in worse shape than before. At that point, everybody's instinct is to yank the second campaign and try a third. And then a fourth. You may end up with a new campaign, but at the grave cost of your brand personality.

The first people to get bored with advertising are, unfortunately, the advertiser and the agency. Not the consumer.

Too many campaigns are discarded before they reach their growth potential. One research study indicated that the average television campaign lasted for only *17 months*. Yet, the same study showed many campaigns continued to build awareness—and sales—*after three and four years*.

If your sales are dropping, the advertising *may* be the root of the problem. But it could be that your product quality has fallen behind its competition, your pricing is off, your delivery system inefficient, or any number of other problems. It could be that your old campaign is doing a heroic job of holding customers. If your brand is in trouble, consider *all* the possibilities—not just the advertising.

Next time you look at a print layout or a storyboard that represents new advertising for your brand, ask yourself if it's merely a brilliant one-shot or the opening gun of a campaign that will last for years.

Visual similarity. This campaign helped move Shell up to second place in gasoline sales.

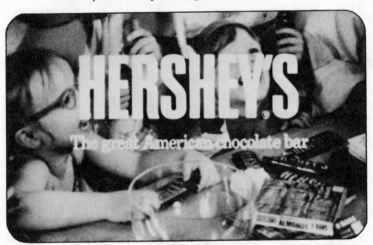

Verbal similarity unites advertising for Hershey's chocolate bar.

A consistent fun attitude built Baskin-Robbins into an international chain of over 1,500 ice cream stores.

Mercedes-Benz in print. A typical long-copy
advertisement that sells engineering, not styling.

Mercedes-Benz in television.
A hair-raising demonstration of
maneuverability.

The visual, verbal and attitudinal
summary of the Mercedes-Benz
campaign.

Chapter VIII

How to Get Better Television Production

THE ROLE OF THE PRODUCER of a television commercial is like that of an orchestra conductor. His job is to carry out the intention of the composer. A great producer can add new dimensions and richness to the original score.

Television production is largely a technical process. You need to understand its basic steps in order to know *what you can do about it*. What danger signals should you look for? How much should it cost? When can you ask for changes?

There are three stages of production:

1. Preproduction—the work that goes on before the day of filming, including casting, estimating costs, legal approvals, production bids, and selection of a production company.

2. Production—the day (or days) of filming or taping.

3. Finishing—the completion of the film or tape.

Preproduction

Only when you have firm and definite approvals, and not before, should you give the agency a go-ahead to start production.

What makes one commercial cost so much more than another? Sometimes you can look at a storyboard and tell that you have an expensive job on your hands. Here are some tips.

14 Factors That Add to the Cost of a Commercial

1. Location shooting

Transporting a cast and crew to a distant location costs money. Even a *nearby* location can mean extra transportation that requires a longer shooting day, and overtime charges.

2. Large cast

The more actors you use, the more you pay.

3. Superstar talent

The fee is almost always negotiated in advance, and separately from the bidding on the storyboard. But superstars are demanding more every year, and you must figure that into your production budget.

4. Night or weekend filming

If you need a supermarket all to yourself, for example, you will have to shoot on a weekend, or at night. That means *double-time* (or even *triple-time*) rates for the cast and crew.

5. Animation

A normal schedule for completed animation is 12 to 14 weeks. If you want your commercial faster, you may have to pay overtime. Even more expensive is a combination of animation with live action.

6. Involved opticals, special effects, stop motion

These effects may make your shooting day longer and costlier. They will definitely add to editing time and money.

7. Location and studio shooting for one commercial

Any storyboard that depicts both indoor *and* outdoor scenes will probably need two days of shooting.

8. Expensive set construction

Elaborate sets, or sets that require more than one room, cost money. It is often cheaper to find a location.

If you are shooting several commercials that use the same set, film them in a group. You can sometimes shoot two simple commercials on one set in the same day.

9. Special photographic equipment

Cranes, underwater cameras or—especially—aerial photography.

10. A second day of shooting

Studios are normally available only on a full-day basis, and crews must be paid for the entire day, even if you need just an hour.

11. Legal requirements

The lawyers and technical people are aware, as everyone in advertising should be, of the basic ruling of the Federal Trade Commission. It actually sounds quite simple. If a commercial *implies* a material fact, the viewer will accept it as truth. *So it must be true.*

No area is more vulnerable than the *demonstration commercial.* If the demonstration suggests to the viewer that something material to the product is happening up there on the screen, it must be happening, *in fact,* in front of the camera. Further, any problems or hardships incurred because of the film medium are *your* problems.

The law now requires you to shoot demonstration sequences *in continuity.* This can be time consuming, and therefore costly.

12. Children and animals

Unpredictable, and often the cause of production delays.

13. A single word or sentence of dialogue

Sometimes you'll see a storyboard that could be filmed without sound, except for a single word or phrase. Paying a sound crew for a full day of shooting is wasteful. It's cheaper to dub a small portion of sound in later during the editing. (More about dubbing later.)

14. An extremely simple, close-up commercial

That's the kind that may need an entire day just to get the lighting right.

Contributions You Can Make to the Preproduction Meeting

The purpose of the preproduction meeting is to agree on everything possible, before the day of filming.

Caution! Do not ask for alternate shots, changes, or additions, unless absolutely necessary.

It may seem simple to ask that one little piece of action be filmed two different ways. But remember that each action has to match what comes before, and what goes after. Your request can mean that the previous scene will have to be filmed to *end* two different ways, and the scene following filmed to *begin* two different ways. This takes a lot of time. And on a set, time means money.

1. The set

If your product has an elegant, expensive image, you will want an up-scale kitchen. If it's an economy, no-nonsense sort of product, you want the opposite.

2. Costumes and props

Again, consider the image of your product. And remember that in a close-up commercial, the props themselves become the set. If the camera is going to spend 60 seconds looking at a salad being tossed, make sure you have the right salad bowl. And the right lettuce.

3. Demonstrations

Do everything possible to make sure it is going to work—*before* the cameras start rolling.

If it's a particularly difficult demonstration, you might ask for a run-through in the studio well before shooting, with the director and the cameraman present to see what happens. This will cost you some money, but is often worth it.

Sometimes the only way to determine whether a demonstration will work on film is to *film* it. A test shooting can be done on 16 mm film or videotape a week or so before the shooting day. It doesn't require a full studio crew, and usually doesn't need sound equipment, so it can often be done for a minimum amount of money. You may find a way to make the demonstration better. You may find that the demonstration won't work at all.

It pays to spend money on test footage.

4. Casting

Casting is the most subjective of all decisions.

Many commercials stand or fall on the actors. Never settle for a still photograph. Many agencies now have videotape facilities, and can play back the actor's audition for you. If not, ask that the actor be called back so you can watch him do the audition. Obviously you won't go to that trouble when a minor role is concerned.

Encourage the agency to cast unusual, memorable actors and actresses.

Finally, casting should be settled *well before* the eve of the shooting.

5. Your product

The label will probably have to be "color corrected"—clarified for filming, with a lot of the small type removed. Make sure the art director knows what can be removed and what cannot.

How is the product used? If your product is more economical than the competition because you only need half a cupful, make sure the actress won't pour in a full cup.

Production Day

If you are on the set, there is only one thing you have to remember: if it looks wrong, or feels wrong to you, assume it *is* wrong. And act on that assumption.

How do you register your concerns? Whom do you speak to on the set? Go through the account executive, or talk directly to the agency producer. Do not talk to the director, the crew, or—worst of all—the actors. Too many cooks create chaos.

The jargon of the set and how to understand it.

"Bells" is just that—three warning bells that sound to tell everybody to be quiet, hooked up to a red light outside the studio door to warn people sound is being recorded.

The sound man calls out "Speed" to tell the director his tape recorder is rolling at the proper speed. The camera then starts to roll, and films the clapboard, on which the number of the take is marked. It's a convenient way for the editor to differentiate all the many takes of the same scene.

The crash of the blackboard marks the starting point for the synchronization of sound, so the editor later will be able to line up the sound with the picture.

The director's signal for "Action" is a cue to the actors. His direction to "Cut" at the end of the scene is a camera cue, really—cut off the camera roll. If the scene has been a good one, he asks for it to be printed, meaning that the negative for that scene will be developed and printed. If the scene isn't usable, he doesn't want to waste the time and money, so it's a "No Print."

84

Some Tips on Film Production

1. Three good takes for every scene.

We have never seen a director settle for less than *two* good takes for any given scene of the commercial.

2. Scenes don't always start where they seem to start, or end where they seem to end.

Particularly with dialogue and action, directors start filming a little ahead of the section they're interested in, and keep on shooting a line or two after it. Experienced actors know this, and tend to put their efforts into the meat of the scene.

3. Scenes are normally shot from several different angles.

If the commercial has a wife saying to her husband, "I can't go to the party. I have a terrible headache," it may require three different camera positions. One will have the husband and wife together, the second will be a close-up shot of the wife alone saying her line, the third a close-up of the husband alone hearing and reacting to it.

4. Scenes without sound are shot last.

Many close-ups, especially those of the product, don't require sync sound, and are saved for the end of the shooting day, after the sound crew goes home. So don't worry that portions of the storyboard are being skipped over.

5. The director must "shoot the storyboard."

He can *add* to the board, but he must not subtract. If you discover that any frame of the board is not being filmed, you are within your rights to ask that it be done, no matter how late it's getting, or how difficult and time-consuming the shot. Many new elements crop up at a filming, and you may find yourself agreeing with the director that a certain scene, shot as boarded, will look terrible. By all means, go ahead and shoot it a *better* way. But most times you should insist that the scene be shot as boarded, too.

A Guide to Film Editing

Finishing a film is like weaving a rug. If you wait to get to the edges before you fix a bad spot in the middle, you'll have to pull out all the threads and start over. And the longer you wait, the more expensive it gets.

1. The rough cut (also known as the work print, or the interlock)

The picture part of the commercial is on one piece of celluloid, the sound portion on another. *Visually,* the commercial is close to its finished form, without such extra touches as dissolves, titles, special effects and *supers*— words superimposed on the film. These are added later during the optical process.

If the commercial is sync sound, like a slice-of-life, you can regard the *sound* as fairly final, too. You may not hear an announcer, or music, or sound effects until later in the finishing process.

What changes can you make at rough-cut stages?

You can change the picture simply by substituting scenes from the existing footage. This kind of change involves only editorial charges for extra time.

If the commercial needs something more—maybe a new scene or a different shot that was never part of the original footage—now is the time to shoot it. This is usually an expensive step, but if the commercial needs that new footage, you don't have much choice.

Who pays for additional filming?

It depends. Normally, a reshoot is done by agreement, with nobody really at fault. Then the advertiser pays for the extra charges. However, if a scene indicated on the storyboard has been omitted without the approval of the client, the agency or the production house might well be responsible for refilming. (There's an unwritten rule, remember; the storyboard must be filmed.)

How about lip-sync sound? Can you change that at all?

Yes, and with more flexibility than you might expect. If you want to add new words, you can hold on a product close-up, or any other person or object, as long as you are off the face of the actor supposedly saying those new words. This kind of change is inexpensive and just means paying for the actor and a recording session. For a change of emphasis or greater clarity in any given line, you can also bring the actor back to rerecord his own words.

If, for some reason, you are unhappy about the voice quality or reading of an actor, there is one other recourse: *dubbing*—having another actor read the words to match the lip movements on the screen. (This method is used all the time in moviemaking, for different language versions of a film.) Admittedly, it's a tricky process, but one that can pull a bad commercial out of the fire. The original actor *must* give his permission; and you *do* end up paying *two sets* of residuals.

2. Sound recording

The announcer records the voice-over narrative. If he is vital to the commercial, ask to hear an audition tape. If he is simply reading a "tag" at the end, you can get an idea of his voice quality by hearing another commercial he recorded.

3. Music

If you are going to pay $3,500 or more to have an original song written, make sure you hear the basic tune before the musicians come into the studio to record the final version. If there is a vocalist—or lots of background singers—get an idea of the sound before recording day. Calling back lots of musicians and singers is *very* expensive.

If the commercial just needs "incidental" music, or if the production budget is tight, the producer may rely on stock music bought from a music house. Again, you should listen to, and approve, the music before it gets integrated with the rest of the sound in the commercial. Caution: Other advertisers can use the *same* stock music.

4. Sound effects

Usually they are ordinary everyday sounds (doors slamming, doorbells ringing, etc.). They add a great deal to the *realism* of the commercial; if they weren't there, you would miss them.

5. The mix

All the different sound elements—the actors' voices, the announcer's track, the music, the singers, and the sound effects—are *mixed* together on one track.

6. The mixed interlock

It's just what the name implies. The sound is all together on one piece of celluloid; the picture is *almost* all together on another. (It still doesn't have any of the optical effects.) But the sound you are hearing is in its finished form.

7. Slop print (also known as a "check print")

Usually you won't see this one, unless an air date is pressing and you're called upon to give your approval with reservations.

This print (usually without sound) is the first one struck from the printing negative, and is used as a first check on the optical effects only. The color is almost always imperfect at this stage.

8. The answer print

So named because it answers the question: "Is the film right or wrong?" Completed sound track and picture, with all optical effects and titles, are combined on one piece of film.

> *A realistic production timetable (depending on the complexity of the shoot) is four to six weeks from start of filming to finished prints. Plus the time before filming—for preproduction, casting, special requirements.*

9. The finished commercial

TV viewers will never see that commercial on a giant screen, with superb stereo sound. Many of them won't even see it in color.

It pays to see your commercial "on system"—on a

television set, more or less the way it will look in real life. Look at it in black and white, as well as on a color set.

You can pay for a half hour of viewing time at a TV station or production house. A growing number of agencies and advertisers now use videotape cassettes to look at 35 mm interlocks and finished film on a television screen.

Be ready to be surprised.

A busy storyboard that's packed with action often disappoints you when you see the finished commercial. It's a matter of "Loved the book, hated the movie," because the film didn't translate exactly what you saw in your own mind.

But the uninvolving storyboard can turn out quite the opposite, once the film medium gives it a life of its own. "Dull" storyboards can surprise you.

You can sometimes end up with a commercial that's much better—or worse—than you expected. If it's bad, admit your mistake and throw it away. You won't save money running a bad commercial.

A Note on Videotape

If you have taped your commercial, instead of filming it, there is little that changes in the preproduction or production phases. One advantage of tape is that you can see it played back right on the set, and know whether it looks good. The other obvious advantage of tape is speed. If you have no complex optical effects, it is possible to shoot one day and be on the networks the next.

You can also benefit from the speed of tape by

shooting on film and finishing the commercial on tape. Some television advertisers are moving to this procedure, because they get faster finishing.

You can take the film you have shot to a videotape studio and do all the opticals on tape. For instance, suppose you have a super that says: "New whitening action." Well, you can see that super larger. Or smaller. Higher or lower. To the left or to the right. In other words, tape gives you instantly what an optical house might take days or weeks to do in so many different variations.

Film versus videotape

If you want to shoot a simple slice-of-life in a simple set, chances are production costs will vary little between tape and film. In fact, tape may be slightly less.

If your commercial calls for *location* shooting, film is often cheaper—especially if the storyboard needs more than one location. The instant replay you get from tape can help to insure results, however, and could save expensive reshooting. And the recently developed light-weight tape cameras make it easy to move about.

Sensitive lighting? Tape people say they can do anything film can do. Many film people don't agree.

Ten years ago, many directors and cameramen understood film better than tape. Now you find top talent in both areas.

Finishing costs can vary. The hourly rate of tape editing is usually more, but includes opticals and titles, which are additional costs in film editing.

The question of distribution is complex. Your media mix—network versus spot—determines whether you'll save money distributing tape or film.

You must still turn to film for some techniques—such as certain types of animation. For sheer *speed*, go to videotape.

The choice of tape or film plays a far smaller part in the overall production costs than the demands of the individual storyboard.

* * * * *

The finished commercial is less a matter of luck than of dogged attention to detail.

You and the agency have spent weeks, or months, working on the storyboard. Yet one critical day—*the day of filming*—decides its fate. Do not settle for "good enough." Good lighting will not save a shoddy set. The greatest director will not be able to coax a performance from an actor who is not right for the part.

Spend three hours in preparation for every hour on the set. Do not depend on technical miracles.

Shooting on location. As the scene is filmed, the action is also recorded on videotape for instant replay.

A location can improve with creative landscaping.

Insert shots—close-ups of the product in use—are filmed separately.

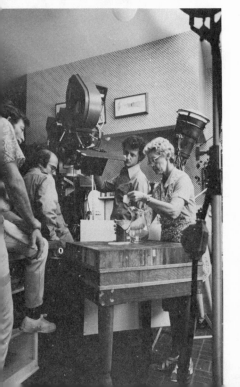

The Moviola projector lets the editor look at the film frame by frame. The sound track is on one set of reels, the pictures are on the other.

Chapter IX

How to Get Better Print Production

I T CAN COST YOU as much to produce a magazine advertisement as a television commercial! Surprised?
Unless you keep a tight rein on costs, it can even run
you more.

Advertisers tend to know less about print production than they do about film; they seldom go to print
"shoots," or peer over a printer's shoulder.

But you can get better production—*and lower
costs*— by understanding print production, and what
you can (or cannot) change along the way.

This chapter will give you a brief guide to production. It will point out expensive mistakes most common-
ly made, and how to avoid them.

It will give you five ways to *cut the costs* of your
print production.

The starting point is a basic technical vocabulary.

Preproduction
As in television, your main role is during preproduction. You have the same process of legal clearances,
technical approvals, and signed estimates. And, whether
or not there is a formal preproduction meeting, insist

upon knowing *explicitly* what the agency plans to do. How will the scene be set for the photograph? *Avoid surprises!*

Two guiding principles:

- *Don't approve anything for production unless you understand exactly what's going to happen, and how much it's going to cost.*

- *The sooner you speak up, the better—and the cheaper.*

A Guide to Print Production

All print production whether for newspapers or magazines follows six basic steps:

1. Layout

A rough sketch of what the advertisement will look like, with the headline lettered in. After preliminary approvals, your agency will usually prepare a more detailed sketch, called a *comp*, or comprehensive layout.

2. Type

The art director chooses the type style, often after consultation with an agency typography expert, and the copy is set. If there is too much copy for the allotted space, you will have to agree on deletions or the selection of a smaller type size. Cutting copy is preferable.

There are hundreds of type styles. Some have *serifs*, that short crossline on the tops or bottoms of certain letters. (This is a *serif typeface.*) Other, more modern typefaces are *sans serif.* (This is sans serif.) Most books, newspapers and magazines use serif styles for their text. Sans serif works better in headlines.

Copy set in lower case is more readable than copy set in all-capitals. That goes for headlines as well as body copy.

Readability is influenced by spacing, between words and paragraphs, as well as type size and style.

Good typography doesn't call attention to itself with self-conscious or distracting design. The reader should not be aware of the type, but of the message.

3. Art

The term *artwork* means any illustration in a print advertisement.

Line art refers to charts, diagrams and illustrations such as simple pen-and-ink sketches. *Tone* art usually means a photograph.

You can look at artwork in many forms—photo prints, color transparencies, or drawings. If you're working with color, you may see a *dye transfer*—the color photograph transferred to a special paper so it can be retouched (although 8" x 10" transparencies can also be retouched).

A good retoucher can make magical changes on a photograph, whether it's changing the Red Sea to green, adding a fig leaf, or subtracting one. Retouching is expensive, but it gives you a flexibility to make changes in print photography impossible in film.

Reproduction of color photography in a magazine is the most complex (and expensive) element of print production. It is based on the use of three primary colors (red, yellow and blue) plus black. This *four-color proc-*

ess printing can reproduce a reasonable facsimile of the photograph.

> *Expect variations in the color reproduction . . .*
> *given the limitations of printing inks, paper stock*
> *and high-speed presses. The color will vary from*
> *magazine to magazine, and from one printing*
> *run to another in a single publication.*

In process printing, four separate plates of the same photograph are prepared, each for its separate color. All four of them must then fit back together precisely for proper color reproduction. If just one of the plates is even a hairbreadth out of line—known as *out of register*—you'll get a blurred picture. (That's another reason for not running type over the color section of an advertisement, but rather keeping it in the clear—with a white background.)

Illustrations can run either with a white border all around the advertisement, or they can *bleed* right off the page—with no border at all. The difference is usually cost; most magazines charge a little extra for bleed. The impact of the bleed illustration is usually worth it.

> *Check some tearsheets to get a feeling of how*
> *much is lost in translation to high-speed printing*
> *runs. In newspapers, even the clearest*
> *photographs can get muddy and indistinct. Poor*
> *reproduction may be grounds for requesting a*
> *rebate.*

4. Mechanical

At this point, you have the headline and body copy set in type. The illustration has been retouched. The final assembly of all these materials is the *mechanical*.

The mechanical is an accurate guide for the position and size of all elements in the advertisement. Insist upon seeing—and approving—the mechanical and final art.

> *If you are going to make any changes, make them now. After this, anything you want to do runs into big money—and time. Artwork should be exactly the way you want it. Don't buy the promise: "We can fix that on the plate."*

5. Platemaking

The production materials now go to the photoengraver, who makes the printing plate (and the *duplicates,* so you can print your advertisement in several publications at once).

Duplicate plates for magazines are metal *electros.* Duplicate plates for newspapers are less expensive paperboard *mats.*

> *For a black-and-white newspaper advertisement, allow one to two weeks from approval of copy to finished plate. For a four-color magazine advertisement, allow five weeks. You can get it more quickly, but you risk overtime costs and poorer reproduction.*

6. Proofs

The first printed version you'll see of your advertisement is a *repro* proof, pulled by hand from a reproduction proof press.

You can request minor changes in color, to come closer to the original art. Thereafter, you'll see *color-corrected* proofs. Next, the engraver will run final proofs on publication stock.

Always evaluate the advertisement on publication stock, not on highly coated papers that don't represent the real world. And always look at it pasted in the magazine—with the big white borders trimmed.

Now it's all in the printer's hands.

Printing

Chances are that you will never have anything to do with the actual printing of your advertisement. But you should know there are four major processes (letterpress, gravure, lithography and screen). Each demands a different preparation of materials. So if you want the same advertisement to appear in two different magazines that are printed by *different methods,* different materials are needed and your costs will be higher.

For this reason at least, you should be familiar with the different methods of printing.

• **Letterpress** is the oldest and most versatile process. Changes in copy can be made at the last minute, which makes it attractive for newspapers and magazines.

• **Gravure** offers the finest reproduction. However, the cost of printing cylinders limits its use to long printing runs—like Sunday supplements and mail order catalogs. (Printing is generally on rotary presses, giving it another name: *rotogravure* or just *roto.*)

• **Lithography** is the fastest growing process. Its good quality and low plate costs are converting many magazines and small newspapers. (Lithography is more often known as *offset,* because the image is printed first on a rubber blanket—then offset onto the paper.)

- **Screen** is the simplest method. It's also the least used because it is not suited for quantity production. However, for transit posters or outdoor boards, it can provide a depth and brilliance of color. (The printing stencil was formerly made of silk, and the process called *silk screen*.)

How to Keep Production Costs Under Control

Special demands will run up your print costs, just as they do in television production. An expensive photographer, location shooting or elaborate set construction, night or weekend shooting, use of children or animals, or special visual effects—all cost extra.

Five Ways to Save Money in Print Production

1. Approve a production estimate before the agency spends any money.

An estimate will identify all the costs for you, and elaborate on any special ones. The basic rule is, "No client okay, no agency activity."

2. Review and approve copy before setting type.

Too often, the body copy is given serious attention only when it gets to the mechanical or plate. There is a strong urge to change things when you realize this is your last chance. Resetting type is expensive. And cutting new type into a plate costs even more. It pays to get all the necessary approvals—including legal and technical okays—while the copy is still typed on paper, not set in type. (Including approval by the agency proofreader.)

3. Ask for a production schedule.

The schedule should outline all activities and due dates. It should alert you anytime you risk heading into the big extra costs of overtime. Get a *realistic* timetable, and try to stick to it.

4. Agree on how you will use the artwork.

When you photograph a subject for a print advertisement, you *buy only the one shot you elect to use,* and for a specified run—unless you agree with the photographer on a *buy-out.*

This is a critical point, since a photographer takes dozens of different angles and exposures. If you want to use *more* than one photograph from the same shooting, you must negotiate. If you go back to the photographer six months later for other pictures, or want them for other uses, you may have to pay more.

5. Check production costs with media.

A media schedule that puts your advertisement in magazines of three different sizes demands printing plates in three different sizes, too. The cost of a new set of plates can turn a good media buy into a bad one. Thoughtful media planning can help. A full page in a small magazine can translate to a junior page in a large one, without a new plate.

* * * * *

Knowing how to get good production won't make a bad advertisement any better. It can help you avoid taking something away from a good one. And save you money.

The layout—a rough sketch for preliminary approvals.

Lighten all clean

Fill in all windows

DARKEN under all edges

Color correct all sides of building

Remove cars and restore grass, add bushes, trees, shrubs

even out curtains & Lighten

Photographs often need retouching.

Chapter X

How to Test an Advertisement

O NE KIND OF advertising research is run by retail stores. "Your reward (or punishment) is immediate," says creative director Reva Korda. "If you've done a workmanlike job, you'll see the eager consumers— noses pressed up against the door before the store opens in the morning. If you haven't, you've got to account for yourself *immediately* to the buyer, and the merchandise manager, and often enough to the president of the store."

If you're not in the retail business and can't read the results of your advertising in the store the next day, you need some other measure of its effectiveness.

This is a guide to how to think about copy testing. Before research can answer your questions, you have to know *which* questions to ask. And *how* to ask them.

The uses of research are far broader than evaluation of a single advertisement. It can help select the best positioning and the most meaningful consumer benefit. It can measure the total advertising campaign.

How to Select the Best Positioning

Spend your research dollars *before* the advertising is written.

Use research to identify your best prospects. Pretest your *strategy*. Pretest your *promise*. Use research to find the best thing to say about your product.

Can you define the target audience clearly? You should be able to answer key questions about demographics, usage patterns and attitudes. The answer is probably in your files, in market reports, or in consumer studies.

If you cannot answer these questions with certainty, *stop!* No issue is more critical than to whom the advertising is directed.

One of the more sophisticated techniques is the segmentation study. It groups consumers into segments on the basis of age, income, product usage, attitudes, needs—or a combination of them.

In order to position its different candy bars, Hershey studied the candy-eating market in terms of consumer attitudes, motivations and purchase behavior.

Hershey positioned Reese's Peanut Butter Cups for kids, who love the combination of chocolate and peanut butter.

Promise testing is a quick and inexpensive technique for determining *what* to say about your product. Different advertising promises are shown to consumers, who are asked to rate them on two criteria: how *important* is that benefit to them, and how *unique* it is.

Group sessions or depth interviews are helpful in generating hypotheses to be tested. But don't rely

105

*only on group sessions. Quantify the results with
a larger sample.*

In promise testing, do include competitive promises but
do not include emotional ones (they need advertising
executions for a fair test). Most of all, make sure your
product can *deliver* the promise you choose.

What the advertising says about your product is
more important than how it says it. *Pretest your strategy.*

How to Select
the Best Advertisement

To be effective, advertising must clearly communicate its message, be memorable, and persuade people to
buy.

Here is a guide to some techniques that evaluate
these dimensions. It deals first with television (which has
the most advanced methods), then with print, radio,
and outdoor.

The first measure: Does it say what you think it says?

You're so close to your product and your advertising, the message is clear to you. Consumers may not understand it; they may misinterpret it.

Communications testing can be done with a filmed
commercial, or even before. One way is in "forced-view-
ing" situations. People are shown a commercial, then
are asked what it told them. This is a relatively cheap
and quick way to probe what the advertising is saying.

A useful tool for copywriters is a small-scale test,

using slides or "animatic" film, to check ideas
before committing to expensive production.

This kind of testing allows you to test the whole commercial, or any part of it—a phrase, a demonstration.

Be sure your commercial really says what you want it to.

The second measure: Is anybody watching?

An advertisement must stop people and make them aware of your product. You can't save souls in an empty church.

The most common tool is the *on-air recall test.* A test commercial is aired in several cities; telephone interviews 24 hours later determine how many people who watched the program remember the commercial.

Recall research is broadly used because the test takes place under in-home viewing conditions, provides a simple score, and is relatively cheap. It also elicits verbatim comments about the commercial.

Unusual or dramatic situations don't assure high
recall. Show how a product is used, or what
problem it solves—not how it is made.
Involvement is more important than impact.

Recall research must be used with an awareness of its *limitations.* It measures only the viewer's ability to remember a commercial—and describe it 24 hours later. Many extraneous factors can influence a recall score. Scores often vary by city, by interest in the program content, by the time of year, and by product category.

Products that are leaders get higher scores than
those with lower market shares. New products
score higher than established brands.

Some of these problems are avoided with a different research method: the *attention* test.

Under the pretext of evaluating television programs, the viewer is given the choice of two channels. One is a low-interest program, the other is a high-interest one—with commercials inserted.

The viewer may switch channels at any time. A line graph records how many people stayed with the entire commercial, and shows—on a second-by-second basis— *where* it lost viewers. An interview after the showing provides some understanding of what the commercial communicated.

The strength of the attention test is its ability to measure how people *behave* (rather than what they remember). The switching pattern is also useful in showing how a commercial can be improved.

The ultimate measure: Is it persuasive?

Persuasion is the most difficult dimension to measure. But the ability to convince consumers to buy is the purpose of all advertising. And it *can* be measured.

There are many techniques for measuring persuasion. Most of them measure in some way the ability of the commercial to change consumer attitudes. For example, an offer of coupons before and after viewing, to check purchase intent. Further questions can uncover the *reasons* for choosing one product over another.

> *Avoid using copy testing to make strategy decisions. You won't know if you're testing strategies or executions.*

Persuasion research is most useful when setting out in an entirely new copy direction. You won't need to do this with every commercial, but at least check the prototype of a new campaign.

Testing print, radio, outdoor

There are several syndicated research services that evaluate magazine readership. If your advertisement is in one of the issues being tested, you can get an indication of how many people "noted" your advertising.

A more controlled technique is to place a dummy newspaper supplement or a magazine with a tipped-in test advertisement in a sample of homes. Readers are asked to evaluate the editorial content.

The interviewer calls back the next day and questions the reader about both magazine and advertising.

Radio commercials are seldom tested, but there is at least one technique available. People are invited to a certain location. While waiting in the anteroom, they are exposed to radio programming that includes control commercials and the test commercial (which is aired twice). Afterwards, the audience is questioned about the commercials.

Alternative outdoor boards can be researched with a *T-scope* (for tachistoscope). This instrument exposes a picture for a precise length of time, and helps test what a poster *communicates.*

The technique can be used for pretesting different outdoor boards, or for post-evaluation.

How to Measure a Campaign

There are two reasons why you need some kind of campaign measurement. First, to determine the impact of multiple exposures of your copy *in the market.* Second, to answer the difficult question of *wear-out.*

Consumer tracking studies can tell you whether your campaign is working. Periodic waves of telephone interviews measure consumer attitudes, awareness and purchase behavior before and during the airing of a campaign. *Changes* in these "soft" measures often predict what will actually happen in sales.

> *Check your competitors, too. A special value of tracking studies is they are one of the few opportunities you get to see how your advertising performs versus your competition.*

The other question—that of commercial *wear-out*—is controversial. It is hard to decide just when a campaign has lost its effectiveness. And falling sales—admittedly a red flag—are not proof that the *advertising* is failing.

Tracking studies help sort out the *reasons* for a sales decline. If attitude ratings are declining, it may be that the advertising has worn out.

What you're really looking for is the most effective campaign at a point in time. Constantly measure your current copy against alternatives. If you find something better, put it on the air.

How to Get Good Research

Here are 15 checkpoints on getting research that you can believe and act on with confidence.

1. Define success in advance.

Before you undertake any research, agree upon what information you need—and what results will constitute success or failure.

> *Should the commercial be judged in terms of recall, persuasion, or communication of a specific copy point . . . and at what level?*

2. Describe the problem.

Give the researcher a clear description of the problem to be solved, not the methodology you think is right. The problem statement is an important (and often neglected) part of any research.

3. Be sure the viewer reacts to the advertising as a consumer, not as an expert.

Disguise the purpose of the interview and the identity of the manufacturer. Don't show rough storyboards, and don't ask people their opinions about your advertising. Get their reactions to your pr 'duct.

4. Get the right sample.

Make sure the testing is done among prime prospects for your product. They may be different from other people.

> *Don't neglect current users. Include them in your target audience.*

5. Get the right interviewing technique.

The cheapest is not always the best. *Telephone interviewing* is fine for short questionnaires (5-10 minutes). *Personal interviews* are the most expensive, but are the best way to conduct long interviews and to ask probing questions that require some thought to answer.

> *Check the interviewer: how many people does each interviewer cover, and does a supervisor do spot checks?*

Mail questionnaires cost the least, but can be unreliable—unless you conduct a special survey among nonrespondents to see if their answers differ.

6. Use several markets.

The differences between cities can be larger than the difference between two advertisements. Test your advertising in several cities, and combine the results.

7. Use the right programming.

On television, use the *same* program if you are testing two commercials. Different programs can mean different scores. Use the kinds of programs that are likely to carry your advertising—sports programs for cars and gasoline, situation comedies for household products.

8. Be careful with market testing of copy.

Before changing campaigns, do validate copy tests by trying the new campaign in a market. You have a base for comparison, and can allow for marketplace variables (distribution, pricing, etc.). But for *new products*, it is better to select advertising based on controlled copy research—and then test a *total* plan in the market.

9. Test the right message length.

Don't test 60-second commercials if :30s are the primary unit in your media plan.

:60s seldom score twice as well as :30s, but may have other values.

10. Remember the score is only an approximation.

If you could interview the *entire* population, you would get a "true" number. Since your score comes instead from a small sample of people, it can range higher or lower than that "true" number. You should know what that *range* of probable rightness is.

Don't think a commercial that gets a score of 16 is necessarily better than one that gets a 14. Always ask how big a numerical difference indicates any real difference in score.

11. Ask how much confidence you can have in the numbers.

Another dimension of statistical variation is the *confidence level.* A 90 percent confidence level simply means that, in nine out of ten times, the same results would be repeated if you did the test among the total population. Once out of ten times, the results might be different. The larger the sample, the higher the confidence level.

You'll want a 95 percent confidence level to change a campaign that is working. A lower level is acceptable if you're just checking a new commercial.

12. Go beyond the numbers.

Lean on the meaning of the numbers. What does the research say about the strengths and weaknesses of the advertisement?

Select the "winning" advertisement not only on how well it scores in research, but on its total strengths. Does it register key copy points? Is the tone appropriate? Does it have long-term campaign potential?

13. Test alternatives.

Force yourself to look for other ways, other advertising solutions. You may be surprised to find that your sure winner turns out to be less effective than another commercial.

14. Make sure copy is the only thing that changes in testing.

Control everything but the advertising. This is not the time to try a new package, a new price, or a new spending level. You'll never know what the copy contributed.

15. Use judgment.

Resist letting the numbers alone dictate a decision. Relate your test results to other research, to the market situation, to your objectives, to which commercial would be a better campaign. And the *verbatims* —what people have actually *said* about your commercial—are key to understanding *why* you got the results you did.

* * * * *

Spend your research time and money early, before the copywriter starts, before everyone gets committed to a strategy or a promise.

Don't use research just to decide: "That's a good commercial; that's a bad one." The best research is research that *leads* you to great advertising.

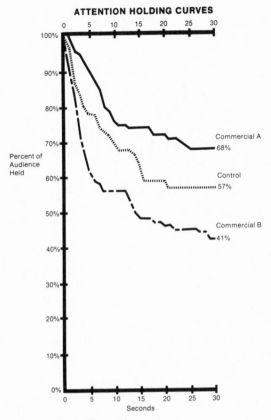

ATTENTION HOLDING CURVES

Percent of
Audience
Held

Commercial A
68%

Control
57%

Commercial B
41%

Seconds

Attention tests measure the holding power of a commercial.

*Commercial ideas can be pretested in inexpensive form
before full production.*

Chapter XI

How to Get Better Media Plans

Mᴏʀᴇ ᴛʜᴀɴ 1,500 messages a day! That's one estimate of how many advertisements are aimed at the average consumer. It boggles the mind!

Suppose it were only a tenth of that. The idea of even 150 messages (every day!) is hard to comprehend. It is clear that how and when—and how often—you place your message is going to make a difference.

There are four areas where your contributions are needed:

- Building consistent *objectives and strategy*
- Knowing how to *look* at a media plan
- Understanding some fundamental media *principles and tactics*
- *Involving* the media planner (and the copywriter) . . . to get better media plans

Like copy, the place to start is with strategy.

How to Create a Media Strategy

The philosophy of a media strategy is simply to put your money where your business is . . . or where you *want* it to be. It's a more precise extension of the marketing strategy.

You can contribute most to the media process in the definition of objectives (what you want the plan to *accomplish*).

Media objectives are built around answers to five questions: who, when, where, how often, and in what way?

Whom do you want to reach?

Describe your audience's *demographics*: their age, sex, income, education, family status, occupation, buying habits.

> *Be precise. Not "primary emphasis on men," but "70 percent of messages directed to men, 30 percent to women."*

If you know their life-style or attitudes ("psychographics"), describe these.

> *Translate descriptions into actionable terms. Not "influentials," but "college education, incomes over $20,000."*

Give the media planner an understanding of how the *decision process* works. Sometimes buying decisions can be influenced by other family members.

> *Families are the best customers for fast-food restaurants. Parents may decide to eat out, but kids usually select which restaurant.*

When do you want to reach them?

Do people buy your product year-round, or primarily in the summer, or on weekends or just when it rains? Some products are keyed to holidays—candy around Halloween, barbecue sauce for July Fourth, or

117

gas for the Labor Day weekend. *Be specific:* what percent of messages should be allocated by quarter, by month or even by the day of the week?

Allocate your media to periods when people *decide* to buy, not necessarily when they make the purchase.

> *The higher the price tag, the longer the lead time.*
> *Travel to Europe peaks in the summer, for*
> *example, but the decision is made in the spring.*

Where do they live?

Geography—whether to advertise nationally or locally—may be the hardest decision for national marketers. *All business is local*—and varies all across the country. Be specific in describing your key markets—and what percent of business they represent.

> *The brand development index (BDI) identifies*
> *your best markets in terms of sales per thousand*
> *population. You may sell more in New York than*
> *Boston, but Bostonians may be better customers.*

Beyond markets, you'll want to identify where your prospects live in terms of county size, city size, suburbs or center-city.

How often do you want to reach them?

The issue of advertising intensity is a complex question we'll discuss later in this chapter. It involves concepts of audience reach and frequency and impact.

Your media objectives, however, should include goals for the *minimum* number of messages necessary to make a sale, and how those messages should be timed.

In what way do you want to reach them?

The best environment for the copy, for example. Does it require color or action? Would it be more effec-

118

tive in a news medium or one that offers service information to women? Should it have an impact on the trade (to get displays) or on employees (to improve morale)? Special considerations like these must be considered as objectives.

Now the media planner takes over.

The planner translates objectives into a media strategy—to say *how* the plan will accomplish these goals.

This is not the plan, but a statement of what *types of media* will be used, when they will run, where and how often.

And *why*. A detailed explanation of these choices, a rationale, is the final ingredient of the strategy.

How to Look at a Media Plan

The place to start is understanding media language. Some terms apply to all media, some apply only to broadcast or print.

Five concepts basic to all media

Cost per thousand (CPM) is the cost to reach 1,000 things, whether households or women or left-handed dog owners. CPM reduces a variety of different audiences, costs and delivery to one common denominator. Always ask "Cost per thousand *what?*"

> *If a television spot costs $60,000 and reaches 12 million homes, the cost per thousand homes is $5.00 ($60,000 divided by 12 million).*

Reach is the number of *different* homes (or individuals) exposed to at least one message over a period of time.

119

*If your media plan gets to four out of five homes,
it has a reach of 80.*

Frequency is the number of times a home (or individual) is exposed to a message—*on average.*

*If six of your messages are seen in four homes, the
frequency is expressed as 1.5.*

(The time period measured for reach and frequency must always be the same, since they are tied together. It is usually four weeks.)

Frequency distribution is an analysis of how the *average* frequency actually distributes over the population, since no home really sees 1.5 messages.

*Some homes receive one message, some two, etc.
The maximum is always the total number of
advertisements run.*

Impressions represent the total number of messages delivered by a media plan, whatever the media used— the number of people who see a message multiplied by the number of times they see it.

Three basic broadcast concepts

Rating is the percent of individuals or homes in the total viewing area tuned to a *particular program.*

*If two out of five homes are tuned to a program, it
has a 40 percent rating.*

Gross rating points (GRP) is the sum of all ratings in your plan.

*If you buy three 40-rated spots, the plan delivers
120 GRPs.*

(With increasing audience selectivity, you may see terms like WGRPs—for "women GRPs.")

Homes using television (HUT) represents the size of the audience available. It is the percent of homes using their television sets at a given hour. This varies by the time of day, the day of the week, the season of the year, and the area of the country.

Television viewing goes up in the evening, and in the winter, raising the potential audience (and cost) for your commercial.

These concepts can apply to radio as well as television.

Four basic print concepts

Circulation is the number of copies of an issue of a magazine or newspaper that is distributed.

Primary audience is the number of readers who get a magazine at a newsstand or in the mail as subscribers. (*Controlled* circulation magazines mail copies free to a selected audience.)

Secondary audience (or *pass-along*) is the number of readers exposed to a magazine other than by direct purchase—in barber shops, for example.

Total audience is the sum of the primary and secondary audiences, all the readers.

Media Principles

How to use reach and frequency

First, use them to determine if the media plan can *achieve the goals* of your strategy.

If your advertising objective is to get 50 percent of homes to be aware of your product or to try it, it can't be done if your reach is less than 50 percent.

Second, recognize that reach and frequency are

interrelated. As reach goes up, frequency comes down. You can't have both unless you add more money or go to a different media plan. Determine the best balance for your objectives.

> *The relationship between reach, frequency and rating points is expressed in this formula: R x F = GRP.*
>
> *If your plan delivers a 90 reach and a 4 frequency, the total GRPs in a four-week period will be 360, or 90 per week.*

Finally, be aware that the same words in different contexts can mean different things. A medium that *reaches* young people or the *frequency* of newspaper advertisements in a schedule is not the same consumer exposure concept expressed in reach and frequency figures.

Two keys to success: frequency and continuity

People's memories are short. That was the finding of a German psychologist, Hermann Ebbinghaus, in 1885. What Professor Ebbinghaus learned was:

- People forget 60 percent of what they learn within a half-day.

- The more repetition, the better retention.

- Forgetting is rapid immediately after learning, and then levels off.

These facts are fundamental to two media issues: first, the relative importance of frequency versus reach; second, the value of continuous advertising.

<u>People forget quickly</u>. Advertisers who seek to reach a broad audience *at the expense of sufficient frequency* among key prospects risk wasting all their advertising.

> *If your product is one that people are always in*

122

*the market for—soap or toothpaste—the need for
"reminder" advertising is obvious. But frequency
is just as important for products purchased only
occasionally—cars, headache remedies. The
message must be there when people are ready to
purchase.*

Repetition aids retention. Most of the great advertising
success stories are ones of *frequency*. Even low-spending
brands usually succeed by concentrating messages
against a select audience.

Don't aim for a broad target with a small budget.
Better to reduce the reach objective and aim for a smaller audience—*with sufficient frequency to be effective*. This
may mean advertising in fewer markets, advertising
some products but not others, or advertising only in vehicles that reach a precisely defined group of people.

Your message needs *continuity* as well as frequency, if it's to be remembered. If money were no consideration, plans would all call for continuous advertising for
52 weeks at high levels.

Since that isn't practical, compromises must be
made between effective levels and budgets.

One is *flighting,* the concentration of advertising
into bursts, with a *hiatus* (no advertising) in between.
The theory is that it is better to be in at meaningful levels for brief periods, four 4-week flights for example,
than to go to lower weekly levels for longer periods of
time. (Flights can also be used to support promotions or
to concentrate funds in key buying seasons.)

The best of both worlds may be *pulsing*—continuous advertising plus periodic bursts—to recognize sea-
sonality, promotions and similar considerations.

Each product's need for frequency depends on its

purchase cycle, its stage of development, competition, and the advertising copy.

How to Get Better Media Plans

Here are nine suggestions:

1. First, establish marketing objectives.

How should the media plan fit with other parts of the business, including the creative direction? Have you given the planner *all* the latest marketing data?

2. Agree—in advance—on media objectives and strategies.

Make sure you understand the *implications* of the need for impact or continuity, minimum reach or frequency goals, the values assigned to magazines or outdoor. Are the objectives *reasonable*, or is the budget spread too thin?

> *Air your prejudices early. What have you learned from past experiences? What special needs should be accommodated in the plan?*

3. Encourage meetings between media and copy groups.

There should be an active understanding of how both work together. The media planner should be at *all* meetings where media is discussed.

4. Make the timetable reasonable.

Schedule work far enough in advance to allow the planner to be thorough and innovative. If there's not enough time, you'll get a plan—but maybe not the best one.

5. Look beyond the obvious.

Why not direct mail instead of newspapers, or radio instead of TV? Can you deliver your message in half-pages instead of full pages, or even 10-second commercials instead of :30s?

But don't look for difference for the sake of difference. Look for what is *right.*

6. Look beyond cost per thousand.

Efficiency is a starting point, but CPM is the weakest evaluation tool. It measures cost, not effectiveness.

7. Recognize that all media plans are a compromise.

Media plans are a *balance between options*—reach, frequency, weeks of advertising, geography . . . and budget. *Don't expect simple answers.*

> *Media is simpler in other countries.*
> *Geographical differences alone are much greater*
> *in the United States. There are far more media*
> *choices here, and media outlets.*

8. Don't lose perspective.

There's a temptation to forget the total media environment, particularly *noise level.* A plan that is the biggest in a category may not dominate a medium.

Don't overread small differences in large numbers when selecting between alternatives. *Stand back and react to the total plan.*

9. Take a media planner to lunch.

It pays to see the media group when there is no problem and no urgent need for a plan. That's the time for updating—and thinking.

125

How to coordinate copy and media

Copy and media plans each start from the same source, but then proceed on separate tracks. If the copy is in conflict with the media recommendation, which gives?

The common problem is a media recommendation based on sound figures and a campaign that doesn't execute well in that medium. Should you have different campaigns for different media?

The answer is *no*, never. Not if the audience is the same.

A good campaign can always translate to some extent to another medium. If it doesn't have a memorable visual or a memorable line or a memorable *idea*, it doesn't deserve to be your campaign.

Suppose there is an impasse between the media plan and the creative idea? *Always give the creative idea the benefit of the doubt.* You run a greater risk of failure with less than the best advertising than with less than the best media plan.

Creativity in Media

The numbers are a guide to media planning. Beyond the numbers there are opportunities to be creative and build *impact*.

For example:

- Open Pit barbecue sauce gained impact in radio advertising to Blacks by sponsoring a *disc jockey contest* for the best live delivery commercial.

- Maxwell House coffee explored new audiences by placing advertising in *paperback books*.

126

- Drāno advertised in the *Yellow Pages* of the telephone book, suggesting that people try Drāno before calling the plumber.
- NoDoz concentrated its *radio spots after 9 P.M.* to reach the tired driver.
- Merrill Lynch established a newspaper advertising position *opposite the stock market tables* to reach investors.

The rewards of impact cannot be judged in terms of efficiency.

* * * * *

You can measure how well the plan meets your objectives. Since it is easier to quantify a media plan than any other part of your marketing mix, you can check the delivery of the plan in terms of the *specific* goals set for it. You can also evaluate a variety of *alternate* plans.

The best media plan is based on clear objectives and early involvement of the media planner—not just in media—but in every part of your advertising.

There's an Arab proverb that says, "When you go shopping for wisdom, visit every tent in the bazaar."

REACH

THE NUMBER OF DIFFERENT INDIVIDUALS (HOMES) EXPOSED TO A MEDIA SCHEDULE.

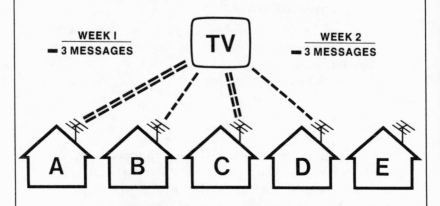

WEEK 1 REACH – 3 OF 5 HOMES = 60%
WEEK 2 REACH – 3 OF 5 HOMES = 60%
TOTAL REACH – 4 OF 5 HOMES = 80%

FREQUENCY

THE NUMBER OF TIMES AN INDIVIDUAL (OR HOME) IS EXPOSED TO AN ADVERTISING MESSAGE.

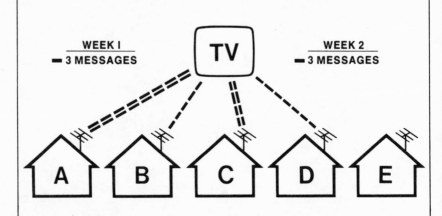

$$\frac{\text{TOTAL MESSAGES} - 6}{\text{TOTAL HOMES REACHED} - 4} = \text{1.5 AVERAGE FREQUENCY}$$

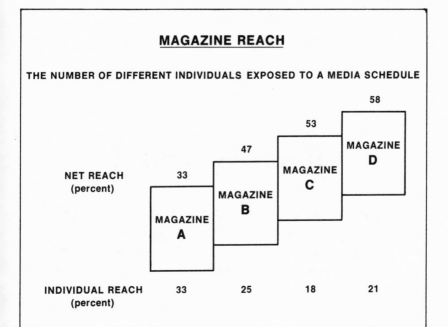

MAGAZINE REACH

THE NUMBER OF DIFFERENT INDIVIDUALS EXPOSED TO A MEDIA SCHEDULE

				58
			53	MAGAZINE D
		47	MAGAZINE C	
NET REACH (percent)	33	MAGAZINE B		
	MAGAZINE A			
INDIVIDUAL REACH (percent)	33	25	18	21

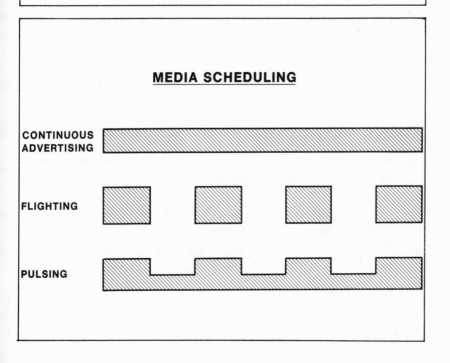

MEDIA SCHEDULING

CONTINUOUS ADVERTISING

FLIGHTING

PULSING

Chapter XII

Truth
in Advertising

ADVERTISING is a highly visible target. Its excesses of *bad taste*—incessant commercial interruptions of programs, billboards located in scenic areas—have been criticized, often with justification.

The *integrity* of advertising is also under fire. A 1969 study showed that 60 percent of the population believe that advertisements *do not present a true picture of the product advertised.* That figure would be higher today.

How truthful is advertising? Do advertisers have a social responsibility?

Thoreau suggests we should aim to do more than just stay out of jail. "It is not desirable to cultivate a respect for the law, so much as for the right."

What is *truthful* is determined clearly by the law. That is the first consideration of advertising.

What is *right* is no less important. Advertising is a powerful communicator of values. It cannot be expected to lead social change, but it must be sensitive to changing values in our society. Advertising does not exist in an amoral environment.

This chapter deals first with the *legal* responsibilities. It then discusses the *extralegal* social responsibilities of communicating to, or about, three special audiences: racial minorities, women, and children.

Advertising and the Law

Advertising regulation did not arrive on the scene with the consumer movement. Most of the federal legislation cited by consumer advocates is over 50 years old.

The Federal Trade Commission seems a new force to be reckoned with. It was actually created by Congress in 1914.

There is a new drive to make advertisers substantiate product claims. Television networks have long required substantiation of claims by advertisers.

Tens of thousands of television commercials have been aired over the past 30 years. Most have told the truth.

So *why* the sudden furor about regulating deceptive advertising?

The answer, in part at least, is that the definition of what is *truth* has changed.

Regulations *are* more stringent, true. But that's only part of the story. Today's consumers are much less tolerant of products that don't deliver—or of advertising that misleads. They expect businessmen to be socially responsible in their dealings with the public.

Here are some broad legal considerations:

1. Tell the truth, show the truth.

In these pages, we have urged you to pay attention to the *pictures*, not just the words, of an advertisement. The lawyers have apparently learned this lesson, for

131

they are paying great attention to what is shown, as well as what is said.

Your product must be shown exactly as the consumer buys it—in all *material* respects. You cannot have product specially selected, or constructed, for use in advertising. Use products straight from your production line.

You must also avoid strange camera angles that make the product look other than it is. You can't use a smaller-than-normal-size cereal bowl to make a portion of your cereal look larger.

If you take a photograph for a whiskey advertisement, with a young man and woman holding glasses of your product, you may not retouch the glasses to make the whiskey appear lighter, or darker. If there is a blemish on the girl's cheek, you can retouch that. Her complexion is *not material* to the sale of your product. Were your product a skin cream, however, her complexion would be important, and you could not retouch.

2. Be sure the general impression is truthful.

Your advertising will be judged, in the long run, by *what the consumer thinks you said.*

> *You are marketing a food product that, eaten with an eight-ounce glass of milk, adds up to a nutritionally balanced meal. Your advertising may mention the glass of milk; it may even picture it. But if the consumer receives the impression that your product, all by itself, delivers complete nutrition, your advertising is deceptive.*

If you have research in hand that indicates consumers are getting the wrong *impression* from an advertisement, you must correct it. If you do not, the Federal Trade

Commission can rule that you are running advertising *deliberately intended to deceive.*

3. Ban "weasels" and dangling comparisons.

"Weasels" are sly little turns of phrase that some copywriters use to get advertising through legal review. "This detergent can give you the whitest wash you've ever seen." The weasel, of course, is the word *can.* The consumer is bound to miss that little disclaimer. All she will hear is the promise of the whitest wash ever.

"This detergent will give you a whiter wash" is a dangling comparison. Whiter than what? You must spell out whether the detergent gives you a whiter wash *than it used to,* or a whiter wash *than competitors.*

4. Substantiate product claims.

Inflated product claims ("the world's most beautiful car") used to be acceptable as mere puffery. Today, the definition of puffery is different. It refers to a *subjective* claim about a product, a claim which really cannot be substantiated. "This is a beautiful carpet." "Great-tasting coffee." "Fried chicken like Mother used to make."

However, as soon as you move into the area of an objective or competitive claim, you must have research that substantiates it. If you want to say your carpet is "more beautiful than the other leading carpet," you must be able to prove that a majority of consumers think so.

5. Testimonials must be backed by research.

You may find a consumer who honestly believes that your cake mix makes fluffier cake than the leading competitor's. However, you cannot quote her in an ad-

133

vertisement without research that proves she is right. Such a testimonial would imply that your cake mix, *in fact*, makes a fluffier cake; your implication must rest on truth.

> *In the American Express Card commercials, if a man says he has used his Card in Rome, the implication is that the Card is widely accepted in Rome. So that must be the fact.*

6. Set up a system of approvals.

Regulate your own advertising. Don't wait for the government to do it for you.

Many agencies now have legal departments. They also, in many instances, check advertisements with outside legal counsel. Large advertisers have their own legal departments. Factual data is also checked by technical or research departments.

> *One large advertiser has a consumer claims review board, which must approve every advertisement. Members represent its research, home economics, legal and corporate departments. Each advertisement is judged, not only in legal terms, but for "the net impression it is likely to make on the general populace."*

An advertising manager must put on different hats when he reviews advertising—one for judging what is *effective*, another for judging what is *truthful* and *socially responsible*.

7. You and your agency are partners before the law.

Who takes responsibility for what is truthful?

You cannot absolve your agency of liability before

the law by assuming that responsibility yourself. You are *both* separately and equally responsible for advertising presented to the consumer. Each of you is considered especially knowledgeable in areas of your own expertise. The advertiser, for example, gives the agency product information which the agency (without its own technical research facilities) accepts as truth. The agency, on its part, is responsible for truthful photography of the product, documentation of demonstrations, and the substantiation of consumer testimonials.

Never ask your agency to stretch the truth.

8. Try to protect the consumer.

Regulatory bodies insist more and more on advertising that protects consumers by telling them what they need to know in order to make a decision to purchase. Various segments of the population need special protection. New rules on nutritional claims and food-ingredient labeling protect the poor. Drug advertising is regulated with special concern for the aged. Toy advertising is regulated to protect children.

Some people believe advertising should tell the public what is potentially *bad* about their products as well as what is good. A credit card, while convenient, can cause you to spend money. Ice cream, while delicious, could make you fat.

Advertising, like many other professions, is a business of *persuasion.* Advertising asks only the same liberties accorded to lawyers, congressmen and clergymen.

More information about products and services is clearly in the public interest. The place to start is on the package itself, with more informative labeling. Long, informative advertisements will be helpful in many, but not all, product categories. If you espouse the "full dis-

135

closure" theory, you might insist that all Army recruitment advertising carry the warning: "May be hazardous to your health."

New regulations by federal, state and city governments, the networks, and the advertising industry itself, are made almost daily. So the checklist above does not attempt to be a definitive legal guide. Keep in touch with the changing regulatory environment. And set yourself high standards of truth.

Minority Talent in Advertising

The first 20 years of television portrayed a society that was lily-white. Advertising did little to vary that image. Today, while some advertisers remain holdouts, the use of Blacks is increasing.

The barriers to integration in advertisements are less bigotry than pragmatism: the desire to appeal to the broadest possible audience, a fear that consumers and trade factors (especially in the South) will boycott Black-associated products, and sheer indifference.

Does the use of Blacks in general advertising alienate whites? A 1972 study of 57 television commercials found *no evidence that the use of Blacks alienates a significant number of white consumers.*

The use of Blacks began as a matter of conscience. Large, responsible companies decided that business must help to solve the underemployment problem of minority groups—both on camera and behind it.

Now there is evidence that the use of Blacks *contributes to believability.* In an integrated society, whites *expect* to see other than their suburban neighbors using advertised products. And using Black actors is more persuasive when you're advertising to Blacks.

Some guidelines on how to use minority talent effectively:

1. Think actively about minority talent.

Unless you consciously work to include Blacks, it won't happen. There's always a reason why *this* particular advertisement isn't right for it: the situation isn't right, it's a test market, "we'll use Blacks in the *next* commercial."

2. Avoid tokenism.

A face in the background or one Black in a group is not wrong, but demonstrates something less than full commitment. The minority talent should have a *major* on-camera role. This can be an all-Black commercial or an integrated situation. If your campaign can't accommodate either, consider a special advertisement.

3. Make it believable.

Show situations that are natural and realistic. These can be either Black-only scenes or those presenting realistic social interaction between whites and Blacks. What is "realistic" is changing faster than you think.

Instant Maxwell House coffee used a commercial involving three girls sharing an apartment. One was a Black. While several viewers commented on "the commercial with the Black girl," there were no negative comments.

4. Avoid stereotypes.

Blacks don't want to be shown in "typical" Black

roles, or those in which they are placed in an inferior position (maids, etc.). Avoid racial jokes (which turn off Blacks) and Black militants (who turn off whites).

5. Use Blacks in Black media.

They are more effective among Black readers or television viewers, say studies by the Newspaper Advertising Bureau and Audience Studies, Inc. (TV).

6. Get help in advertising to Blacks.

There is a distinct subculture that can be turned off by inappropriate language or settings. Black advertising specialists can help you create more persuasive copy and prevent embarrassing blunders.

> *"The Black consumer market is changing rapidly," says Kelvin Wall of The Black Creative Group. "The current practice of relying solely on Black models or ethnic Black language is now outmoded."*

The use of minority group talent can be founded on solid business reasons, whether you have a product that appeals strongly to this market or has only average usage. But the ultimate reason is one of conscience.

Advertising and Women

There has been no legislation to guide the use of women in your advertising, but certainly women's groups are lobbying for it. Advertisers are aware of pressure to eliminate stereotypes of women: woman as drudge, as sex symbol, as shrew, or even as happy little homemaker.

1. Be aware of women's roles in your advertising.

Perhaps the nature of your product demands that you show a woman in the kitchen. Even so, there may be some way you can enhance her situation.

> *The National Organization of Women scolded Dove for Dishes advertising because it always showed women washing dishes, never men. However, the product's positioning was based on a promise of soft, smooth hands. The next commercial offered a partial solution: a husband who was drying the dishes. Favorable consumer letters followed, and the helpful husband became a fixture of Dove commercials.*

2. Recognize that women's attitudes are changing.

Advertising cannot serve as a tool of the liberation movement, but it can mirror the change in women's roles and attitudes. They *are* changing. And not just in New York and Los Angeles. The editors of *Ms.* magazine believe the women most receptive to change are not young, urban Easterners, but middle-aged Midwest housewives who have never held a job.

3. Admit the existence of the working woman.

Your media plan, if not your advertising, should acknowledge the *working* woman. Statistics show that over 50 percent of working-age women now hold full-time or part-time jobs. The number grows every year. And the increase is due to the numbers of *married women with children* who are returning to—or discovering—careers. The nonworking mother is in the minority.

The working woman tends to read fewer magazines, more newspapers. She watches television less fre-

139

quently, but more intently than her nonworking sister. She has additional income to buy convenience foods, appliances—anything that will make her life easier.

4. Avoid stereotypes.

The National Advertising Review Board suggests several questions that will help you.

> *Does the advertisement portray a "dumb blonde,"*
> *a nag, a compulsive cleaner, a vamp? Is it trying*
> *to arouse insecurities: disapproval by a husband*
> *or mother-in-law? Does it show a woman in a*
> *positive role—making decisions, enjoying a*
> *career, as an equal partner in her home?*

To portray women more fairly, you must think actively about their roles. How would you feel if *your* daughter grew up to act like the woman in your advertisement?

Advertising to Children

The world of children's advertising is one of do's and don'ts. Regulation is not new; the toy companies have been operating under guidelines of the National Association of Broadcasters for ten years. But there are new rules coming, and they go beyond toys.

Children are heavy viewers of television. They watch it every day (not just Saturday) and a good part of the night. In fact, according to Nielsen, children watch more *adult* television than children's television.

TV is an especially persuasive medium among children under ten, who are less able to distinguish between fantasy and reality. So the primary thrust of the new regulations is to make sure that advertising *does not exploit younger children.*

Most of the prohibitions cover some obvious concerns: distortion of a product's performance; social acceptability (making friends) as a reason for using a product; encouragement of eating habits (snacks) that could interfere with good nutrition.

You can still create advertising for children that is effective—*and* socially responsible, despite all the many restrictions.

Advertising to children is a special art, which has evolved its own creative rules. Here are seven important ones:

1. Kids are the best means of creating advertising for kids.

Watch and listen to today's children, and talk to them in terms of *their* experience, not your own memories of childhood. Children like products that make them feel grown-up. They love products that let them put on the adult world.

Cast children carefully. Children emulate older children. When in doubt, cast older. Girls emulate boys, but boys don't emulate girls. When in doubt, cast boys.

2. The children's market is not one, but three.

The one-to-five-year-old preschoolers rely most on parental decisions. The six-to-nine-year-olds are faddists, and the heaviest watchers of television. The 10-to-13-year-olds emulate teenagers. (Of course, children have different growth rates. These are only rough guides.)

3. The commercial is the product.

Young children don't discriminate between adver-

141

tising and what is advertised. The product must live up to the advertising.

> *Children take you literally. You can no longer say "You and your doll can take a ski trip" but "You can pretend you and your doll are taking a ski trip."*

4. Don't be overly concerned about wear-out of commercials.

Children have their favorite commercials; they love to see them repeated.

5. Create a personality for your product.

A personality will help keep kids loyal to your product. Once they have made a decision, they won't be switched.

> *Probably the most famous children's personality ever created was the Barbie doll. At the height of her popularity, Barbie was getting 10,000 letters a week—more than any television or motion picture star.*

6. Kids respond to the promise of fun.

Make your product fun—and make your advertising funny. Children love broad humor, especially if the commercial makes fun of grown-ups.

> *A Hershey commercial made drinking milk fun, by having a herd of cows march on a city when they heard the kids weren't drinking their milk. The solution: Hershey's Instant "gives milk that super Hershey taste."*

7. Reassure parents about your product.

If it is a toy, how safe is it? If it is a food, how nutri-

142

tious is it? Your agency assumes that your toy has been made to be as child-proof as possible, and that you've considered how your food fits into a child's eating habits. Tell the parents about it.

Children are a special audience, points out Federal Trade Commission Chairman Lewis Engman. They do not react to programs or commercials in precisely the same way as adults. Chairman Engman warns: " . . . if television advertising deceives our children, if it frustrates them through false or misleading promises, if it promotes the sale of dangerous toys or other products, if it fosters dietary habits which endanger their health— if it does these things, I think television advertising will soon find itself circumscribed by legal restrictions and requirements."

Television advertising is already circumscribed to a considerable extent—especially in the area of talking to children. As a section of the population who cannot speak for themselves, children do deserve some special protection.

To what extent should advertisers protect children? Should we be selling to them in the first place? There is little evidence that children's advertising has any ill effect.

The ultimate solution is not in banning children's advertising, but in making sure that advertising talks responsibly to *all* audience segments—including children.

* * * * *

We like to believe that, while laws change, moral standards remain constant. Actually, *the opposite is true.* It's hard to remember now the shock that greeted the first mini-skirts. Concepts of sexual permissiveness have changed dramatically in the past ten years. "Appropriate" family roles have been altered with the rise of working women. Equal opportunities in education, jobs and housing have long been law, but only recently accepted in practice.

Regulations governing advertising have changed little over the past ten years; the ethical interpretation of them is dramatically different. We look with different eyes at practices that seemed reasonable then. Special preparation of a product for filming. Claiming "more cleaning power" on the basis of one percent more cleaning ingredient. Or searching for legal language that shades the truth. No more. Our sights have been raised.

New evidence renders "truth" of the past fallacious. "What everybody echoes as true today," said Thoreau, "may turn out to be a falsehood tomorrow."

Advertising is now scrutinized with a different perspective of truth than it was a few years ago. As ethical standards change, so does the advertising created within them.

Advertising is a business of *persuasion*. Within the context of its times, it must be truthful and responsible.

The law. If testimonials imply the American Express Card is widely accepted in Rome, that must be the fact.

Minorities. Viewers had no negative reaction to a commercial showing a Black girl sharing an apartment with two white girls.

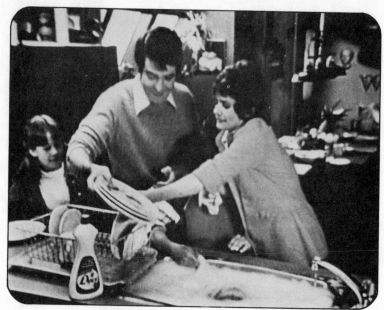

Women in advertising. Helpful husbands have become a positive fixture in Dove for Dishes commercials.

Advertising to children. Barbie doll got 10,000 letters a week at the height of her popularity.

Chapter XIII

How to be a Better Client

T HERE IS ONE revelation that should be clear to you by
now: *the advertising you get from your agency depends
on you.*

When you look at a storyboard or a print advertisement, it helps to know what usually works and what
doesn't. The *interpretation* of these principles is highly
subjective—your personal reactions and those of your
agency partners.

What do you look for in an agency, if you don't
have one (or are unhappy with the one you have)?

How do you work most effectively with the agency
you have chosen?

The answers to both questions may be the most
important ingredients of a great advertisement.

How to Select an Advertising Agency

It's like getting married, without much chance for
courtship. No two advertising agencies are exactly alike;
one will be a better partner *for you.* Choose as though

you were going to live together for the rest of your lives.

Too many advertisers make *size* a major issue. Large or small, any agency will give you about the same number of people working on your account. Maybe you need only *part* of an agency. You can do that too. Agencies will often provide media planning, buying, or creative services on an "à la carte" basis.

Creative "boutiques" and *new product specialists* are small agencies with a speciality. The "boutique" emphasizes creative services. Its size gives you the advantage of working directly with the principals (at least until it grows bigger). The new product agencies—creative-marketing teams—develop positionings and concepts.

How about *specialized* agencies? Some concentrate on semi-technical subjects— industrial, agricultural, medical or financial. They can give you instant knowledge of a complex market. However, you may find similar expertise in a non-specialized agency, along with a fresh approach to the problem.

For most advertisers, *full-service* agencies provide significant benefits. Advertising is more than just advertisements. It is a *process* of business analysis, strategic thinking, testing, and creative execution.

Here are eight guidelines to help you select the right partner:

1. List your needs.

Define your problems; at the very least, state your symptoms. Put them in writing, and get agreement from all your key people who will have a say in approving the advertising.

What is your policy on an agency handling products that may compete with yours? Many

advertisers have begun to look the other way on
minor conflicts. The security issue is usually
overstated.

Tell your current agency *now* that you have decided to make a change, and explain why. Don't ever let it dangle, or place it in competition with a potential new group.

2. Do your homework.

Pull together a short list of agencies whose point of view you respect, and who have an affinity for your business. People can come and go; you want an *organization* that specializes in advertising.

Look for a business philosophy, stable
management, a professional staff, technical
expertise, and a past, present and future.

3. Go see the agencies on your list.

Lengthy questionnaires won't tell you what you need to know. Meet the people who would actually work on your business, as well as the principals. Spend time with them informally—and individually, not just in conference rooms. Personal chemistry is important. Beware of new business teams who woo your account, then turn it over to other people.

4. Select a few finalists.

Meet with them (always separately), and tell them all they need to know about *you.* Don't make them waste time researching the basics. You want them to concentrate on your problems, and consider how they would solve them.

Formal presentations are not always necessary.

149

You seldom learn anything of consequence at
these carefully rehearsed performances.

What you want to know about each agency is what resources it has to offer, and how these will be brought to bear on your business.

5. Be discreet.

Brace yourself for publicity, rumors and calls from friends. There is no way you can prevent it. Avoid gossip and leaks to the press that add grist to the mill. Assure potential new agencies that you are a serious buyer, not a window shopper.

6. Don't ask for speculative copy.

The best advertising comes from a deep understanding of your business—usually after many months. And think about it. Once it's *your* agency, you wouldn't want it to expend creative time and talent on somebody else's new business presentation, would you?

Look at the agency's creative work as a consumer
would. Don't have it paraded before you with
lengthy explanations.

7. Evaluate the finalists against your needs.

Encourage informal presentations, dialogue, frank analysis of your problems. At this stage, questions are better than answers.

Be on guard against the shallow and the
superficial—quick solutions, easy promises,
overwhelming eagerness.

8. Check out your first choice.

Get a financial report. Talk about money. Ask about the ownership of the agency.

It pays to talk to other clients of the agency.
Include former clients.

Like a marriage, a client-agency relationship has its irritations as well as its rewards. Divorce should be a last resort, not taken lightly.

20 Ways to be a Better Client

The other part of the partnership is *you*. The more effective you are as a client, the better the work you will get from your agency.

1. Look for the big idea.

Concentrate first on positioning and brand personality. Too few products have either. Do not allow a *single* advertisement—no matter how brilliant—to change your positioning or your brand personality.

2. Learn the fine art of conducting a creative meeting.

Deal with the important issues first. Strategy. Consumer benefit. Reason-why. State clearly whether you think the advertisement succeeds in these areas. And if not, why not.

> *Creative consultant Bill Tyler says: "My rule of thumb is simply to head right straight into the basic selling proposition immediately following the presentation of any given advertisement. To refuse to comment on the technique, the choice of personalities, the interesting opening, the dramatic close, the tone of the copy, the casting, any of these. Go right for the jugular. Is this a strong selling idea—period."*

3. Cultivate honesty.

Tell your agency the truth. Make sure your advertising tells the truth, and *implies* the truth as well. And never let creative people get away with excuses that honesty is "dull."

4. Be enthusiastic.

When you like the advertising, let the creative people know you like it. Applause is their staff of life. After a really good presentation, send the copywriter a note. You may be amazed at the results.

Be frank when you *don't like the advertising.* Copywriters won't hate you for turning down an idea, if you give them a *reason.* They may even agree with you.

5. Be human.

Try to react like a person, not a corporation. Be human enough to laugh at a funny advertisement, even if it is off-strategy.

6. Be willing to admit you aren't sure.

Don't let your agency press you by asking for the order *immediately* after a new copy presentation. You may need time to absorb what they've been thinking about for a long while.

7. Be consistent.

Try to set a consistent direction for your agency to follow. Every time you change course, you lose some creative momentum. Tack too often, and you lose the race.

8. Insist on creative discipline.

Professionals don't bridle at discipline. A strategy

helps creative people zero in on a target. But remember that rules are only a *starting* point.

9. Keep the creative people involved in your business.

Successful copywriters want to know the latest market shares just as much as you do. Tell them what's happening, good *and* bad. Sales figures, consumer letters, a crazy idea from your research chemist—all can help.

10. Don't insulate your top people from the creative people.

Agency creative people want to receive objectives *directly*—not filtered through layers. While most projects need not involve your top management, a valuable perspective can be provided by those not tied up in the day-to-day work. Good work is done in an atmosphere of involvement, not insulation.

11. Simplify the approval process.

Multi-level copy presentations, often with contradictory direction at each level, can lead to demoralized creative people and bad advertising.

> *The longer the approval process, the more opportunity to make those "little changes" that can ruin an advertisement. A few extra words may seem trivial, but they can overload the commercial and blur your message.*

12. Make the agency feel responsible.

Be a leader, not a nitpicker. *Tell them what you think is wrong, not how to fix it.*

*The best clients are not meddlers. They point
out major problems, and let the agency find
the solutions. "Creative clients" end up with
halfway efforts. The agency expects so many
changes, it won't try very hard on original
submissions.*

13. Don't be afraid to ask for great advertising.

Let your agency know you have confidence in
them to deliver more than just "good solid advertising."
Aiming for greatness involves trying new directions—
and some risks. It is *safer* to go for singles than home
runs. Sometimes the situation calls for more.

14. Suggest work sessions.

Set up informal give-and-take discussions, where
copywriters can air rough ideas, and you can talk about
your objectives. These sessions are especially helpful
just before the agency starts a complex assignment, or if
you have a creative problem to straighten out. *This approach won't work unless you build an atmosphere of confidence. It's not easy to do.*

15. Set objectives.

If you expect action and results, you must know
where you want to go. Set objectives—for your advertising and your business. The secret of management was
stated clearly by Robert McNamara:

> *"The first requirement is to determine your
> objective. Admittedly, it sounds simple and
> obvious to say it, but it isn't. Many businessmen,
> and certainly many public officials, do not have a
> clear concept of what their objective is.*
>
> *"And a second requirement is to measure your*

154

progress toward the object, and not to delude
yourself as to whether or not you are
accomplishing it."

16. Switch people, not agencies.

Candor prevents minor disagreements from becoming major rifts. If there are problems, ask for new people to work on your account. A different copywriter or account executive on your business may provide a fresh approach, without depriving the business of necessary continuity.

17. Be sure the agency makes a profit on your account.

Clients who demand more service than the income can cover are shortsighted. The agency can't afford to put its best people to work on that account and may end up looking for a profitable new account to replace it. In a good relationship, the agency grows as the client grows.

18. Remember that the consumer is changing.

Chances are that the woman who buys your product is not just sitting at home. She is likely to be a *working* mother. She may not believe in Women's Lib, but she is definitely liberated. She may not think of herself as an "environmentalist," but she has been brought up to care about her environment. She may have very different opinions about a lot of things—marriage, child raising, the best way to spend her leisure hours. Advertising that worked ten years ago may not work today.

19. Avoid insularity.

Don't isolate yourself with the same people—at work, on the tennis court, at cocktail parties. Force yourself to go beyond the comfortable world of your own life-style.

> *Get into the field. Visit stores. Talk to buyers,*
> *store managers, stock boys, consumers. Do some*
> *consumer interviews, attend group sessions,*
> *travel with an Avon Lady. Catch a cold and*
> *watch a whole day of television.*

20. Care about being a client.

Creative people do their best work on accounts they like, for clients they like to work with. *Good clients.* That doesn't mean *easy* clients.

There is even competition within an advertising agency to work for certain clients. That's why good clients wind up with the best writers and the best account executives.

The guidelines in this book are a *starting* place. They do not guarantee great advertising. That demands creative brilliance. Hard work. And the understanding of a professional client who knows what works, what doesn't—and why.

Behind all great advertising is a great client.

The authors are officers of Ogilvy & Mather Inc., the ninth largest U.S. agency. Mr. Roman is a senior vice president and account management supervisor; Mrs. Maas is a vice president and creative supervisor.

They thank their agency colleagues for unstinting donations of time and talent. And their clients, from whom they have learned so much.

The following are registered trademarks: